SO YOU
HAVE TO
TEACH
YOUR OWN
MUSIC

SO YOU HAVE
TO TEACH
YOUR OWN MUSIC

Mary Beckwith

PARKER PUBLISHING COMPANY, INC.
West Nyack, N.Y.

PRINTED IN THE UNITED STATES OF AMERICA
13—815407–4 B & P

Why I
Wrote This Book

Music is a child's rightful heritage. He is entitled to a good music program in school and should take an active part in it.

Yet music is a subject often shortchanged. When time is lacking, it's the music period that is skipped, not math or science, not reading or art. Why?

Could the reason be that we secretly feel the loss won't show as it might in other areas? Could it be that we feel inadequate to teach a subject in which we've had little training and little experience?

Music educators estimate that more than 50 percent of all elementary teachers are expected to carry their own music program despite a possible lack of interest, musical background or training. The result is that many children never discover the joys of music—never know how much fun it can be and the satisfaction it brings. Only a fortunate few enjoy the luxury of a comprehensive, continuous, well-planned music program from kindergarten to junior high school.

An effective teacher wants to do the best he can for his children in all areas of study. If the school has a good music program underway, he sees that his class enters into it wholeheartedly and contributes to it. If a planned program is lacking, he starts with his own group.

Teachers have a challenging opportunity to put music across, to en-

courage each child to participate in the creation of an enjoyable, satisfying experience.

This book will show that you *can* teach music to your own class. You
may not be musically talented, you may feel very inadequate, you may
be plain scared. But you *can* give your children what is rightfully theirs
and, perhaps surprisingly, you will have a good time doing it.

MARY BECKWITH

Contents

Part Two: NOW THAT YOU HAVE MORE CONFIDENCE

Part Three: PUTTING MUSIC TO WORK IN THE
CLASSROOM

In Conclusion   210

SO YOU

HAVE TO

TEACH

YOUR OWN

MUSIC

Part One

WHERE DO

YOU BEGIN?

In a world that changes with such incredible speed, the enjoyment of music is one of the few old, reassuring experiences left to us. We can still turn to the familiar folksongs and the timeless symphonies, for they never let us down. Those of us who learned to love and appreciate music when we were children have an inner citadel of satisfaction and security.

What about children growing up in a world so different from anything we knew at their age? Here's one who is sadly deprived and may possibly turn to violence to get what he thinks society owes him. Another is catered to—every wish fulfilled—and he accepts this as his right. In either case he unknowingly yearns for something solid and good and enjoyable that he can call his own.

If you as his teacher could make him such a gift, just imagine what it would mean.

But what can a teacher do?

There's a great deal you can do. You don't need to play an instrument like a Horowitz or a Menuhin to help a child glow with pride when he hears or sings the music of his people—

music that was an expression of their joys and frustrations. You don't need the speed and agility of a top Dixieland drummer like Louis Barbarin to give a child a chance to pound a drum. You don't need to know much about the intricacies of trumpet playing to introduce children to the exciting rhythms of the Tijuana Brass. *You* can give a child pleasure and satisfaction and make him a gift that is his forever—and you can have a good time yourself. Music can become the best part of the school day for you and your class.

chapter 1

Start Simply by
Introducing Rhythm

There is rhythm in Nature, rhythm in poetry, rhythm in painting. It has been called "the heartbeat of music." Primitive man felt the joy of it as he pounded a stick on a hollow log. His tribe knew the joy of it as they moved to the beat and danced to honor a hero or prayed for rain or asked their gods for success in the hunt.

A footsore marcher, whether boy scout or soldier, finds the next mile easier when someone starts a song. Plantation hands sang as they worked. In some instances one of the laborers with a good voice might be relieved of the more onerous tasks if he had the ability to keep field hands working rhythmically to his song.

Cowboys sang to the dogies and managed to get the herd to market. Railroad gangs pounded spikes to the rhythm of a song—and the nation was joined by rail.

Rhythm is completely natural

A child is born with an innate sense of rhythm. See him wave tiny arms and feet as Mother hums to him. See how a child of six months beats his spoon on the high chair when he hears a radio. Did you ever notice the one-year-old's absorption with a TV singing commercial—

the way he holds on to the bars of his playpen and stamps, swings and laughs with joy?

Here is your answer from old Mother Nature herself—"Rhythm! Start with rhythm!"

Capitalize on this innate sense of rhythm

A kindergarten teacher knows the secret. Her children learn to skip, run, "fly" or walk in time to the beat from the piano. They learn how to change from "walking in the park" to "marching in a parade" as the teacher varies the rhythm. Some respond more quickly or more gracefully than others, but each one enjoys the freedom of movement and the opportunity to express himself.

Recently I had the pleasure of observing two little tots at different times and places—neither was more than two or three years old. One was at the Scotch Games in New Brunswick. He held tightly to his parents' hands and as the pipes were sounding, marched along bouncing his kilt that scarcely concealed a diaper. The other, a tiny girl listening to a visiting Dixieland band at a county fair, was doing a pretty good rock and roll in front of a TV camera.

Not all children can express themselves rhythmically at such an early age. Some are naturally quiet and others are awkward when they move but the urge is there and it's up to us to bring it out.

What happens to children when they leave kindergarten where they were relatively free to react and express themselves? Some overall change seems to take place. As they advance through the grades, there is a kind of stifling of spontaneity—a reluctance to let go and try something new. Perhaps in teaching them music we can supply the catalyst that brings a child's natural spontaneity to life. You will find that beginning again with rhythm is the answer.

You don't have to be an expert

There's no big secret to teaching rhythms. If your children are small, their rhythmic movements must be large and simple, for little muscles are untrained. As children grow, they are able to control their muscular activities and can perform more complex rhythms.

If you are uncertain what your class is able to do, start with the large, simple movements. You will know very soon what their abilities are. It is important that *you* relax and perform with the class. Learn as you teach, and you will find that you enjoy it. Unbend physically and mentally when you teach any kind of music. Your class doesn't expect perfection. Laugh away mistakes, and you and they will learn together. This is true whether the class imitates the lumbering gait of an elephant, claps out the beat of "Skip to My Lou" or goes through the motions of conducting a band.

Never mind the grade. If ten-year-olds have been deprived of a comprehensive music program, start with simple rhythms—for you have to start somewhere. When you have their interest and confidence, you can progress as rapidly as you wish.

Often a comprehensive music program is lacking

Some lucky children attend schools where good planning and good music books have combined to provide a continuous, effective music program through the grades. This is the aim of music educators everywhere, but they realize that it's not an easy goal to achieve and it will take time and money. Local school boards will have to be persuaded that music is vital to a well-rounded education.

In some instances the planning has been done, money spent for good books and up-to-date equipment, but the most important ingredient is missing—teachers trained in music, and teachers willing to learn.

It's easier, of course, when children are very young. Kindergarten children laugh and dance and sing with their leaders, and first grade teachers find it relatively easy to continue the program of spontaneous enjoyment. But suppose in second or third grade the class goes to a new teacher who says, "Music? Sure, when I have time. First I must teach some reading and math." You and I know that the time for music will never arrive. So seize any opportunity as it presents itself. An alert, imaginative teacher will find many unexpected, unusual occasions where music in some form or other is the natural answer to a situation.

Let's see how Miss Jacobs handled the problem when a third grade came to her after missing an entire year of planned music training.

"How can I get my children to sing?"

Miss Jacobs is no musician, but she's a dedicated teacher willing to tackle any problem as it arises. When this particular class came along, she knew her hands would be full because, due to a series of unfortunate events, they had been taught by one substitute after another. No matter how efficient substitutes may be, the class discipline and its skills suffer from a frequent change of teachers. Miss Jacobs had few qualms about her ability to teach neglected skills and improve the discipline, but she found any attempt to "teach singing" was met with apathy.

After one exhausting session with some much needed math drill she looked at her drooping pupils and more or less in desperation exclaimed, "Oh, for goodness sake, children, let's have a stretch!" And stretch they did, with sighs of relief.

"Stretch again while I count 1 ———— 2 ———— 3 ———— 4 ————. Now you count with me 1 ———— 2 ————."

Little Steve stood up, yawning and stretching. His yawn seemed to

have three notes in it ♪♩♩ and some of the children laughed.

"That sounded like a song, Miss Jacobs. Listen!" ♪♩♩

Miss Jacobs not only saw the humor of the situation—she had an inspiration. Turning to the board, she quickly sketched three notes.

♪♩♩ "Is that your song, Steve?"

Steve agreed that it was.

"Let's sing Steve's song," said the teacher. And the class tried it with some stretching and a good deal of giggling.

"I know some good words for that song," offered Lillian. "Gosh!

I'm tired!" ♪♩♩

"And I can add three more words," said Miss Jacobs. "Let's all

stretch!" (repeating the same three notes) ♪♩♩

Now the song on the board began to look interesting. The class sang it again and again, and Miss Jacobs was delighted to see the smiles and the interest in this little success.

"Our song needs something else," declared Anne. "It sounds like half a song."

♩ ♩ ♩ ♩ ♩ ♩

"I know," said Jim, "how about this, "Now do you feel bet - ter?"

Miss Jacobs sketched the song on the blackboard, and there it was! Their own song! A completely unforeseen and unplanned class cooperative venture.

The next morning the children wanted to sing it again and again, and Miss Jacobs gladly went along with them. It was just a simple little song, but it came from the natural rhythm of an ordinary, everyday, big, relaxing yawn.

This might be a satisfactory ending for our story but for several things that happened. Miss Jacobs didn't know much about writing music on staffs with time and key signatures. She *could* do it but felt help was needed, so she enlisted the aid of Mrs. Taylor, her partner on the grade, who had more musical background.

Next morning when the class entered the room, there was a fine big sheet of cardboard on display in a prominent place. On it was "The Stretching Song" in all its glory.

The Stretching Song

Then the exclamations and the questions began:

"Is this *our* song?"

"It looks so important!"

"It's just like a song in a regular music book."

"My sister can play music like that."

"What's this funny thing, Miss Jacobs?" (pointing to the G clef).

"Why are there numbers (4/4) near the beginning?"

There was plenty of interest and excitement. First Miss Jacobs asked the children to sing the song as she pointed to the words and notes. Then she talked briefly about such musical terms as staff, clef, time signatures, but only briefly as a sort of friendly introduction to more involved music study.

Miss Jacobs knows she's not an accomplished musician but now she feels more confident of her ability to do something worthwhile in music for her children. Already a list is taking shape in the teacher's plans— a list of ways in which their own song can be used as a stepping-stone:

1—Learn syllable names (do, re, mi, fa, sol, la, ti, do).

2—Sing it as a round.

3—Use resonator bells and triangle for an accompaniment.

4—Recognize the Key of G in which the song happened to be written.

5—Use music readers to find other songs in the same key.

6—Practice singing syllable names of other songs in the same key.

7—Learning value of half and quarter notes.

8—Singing triad chords of their song:
        sol   do
        mi   sol
        do   mi

There is another interesting development connected with this class project (for that's what it has become). Anne, who earlier suggested it sounded like "half a song" still was unsatisfied. After a day or two of experimenting with the resonator bells she came up with the idea that the question, "Now do you feel better?" needed an answer, "Yes, I feel much better."

Coming straight down the scale seemed the best way to answer a question so the song now has a different ending and a new name:

The Complete Stretching Song

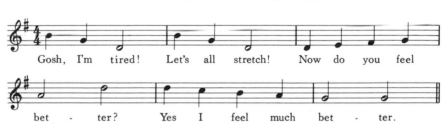

Gosh, I'm tired! Let's all stretch! Now do you feel bet - ter? Yes I feel much bet - ter.

Too much concentration on this creative effort would become boring. Miss Jacobs knows that but there was no problem, for the children's interest in music was at a high peak.

Teachers must be ready to recognize an opportunity, whether it's in music or in other fields. Miss Jacobs has little training in music—and she's not much of a singer—but she's alert to an unusual opportunity. This joint venture has opened the door to (1) creative writing of music, (2) reading music, (3) class singing, (4) simple accompaniments and (5) part singing (of the round).

Another teacher might have found such an opportunity in the study of Indian life: (1) rhythm of Indian drums, (2) five-toned (pentatonic) Indian chants, (3) simple Indian dances.

The sounds of construction in one neighborhood—sounds that had been disturbing the usual routines—became the basis for a class study of sounds and rhythms.

Sometimes a child becomes fascinated with the flowing rhythm of a poem which becomes the lyric for an original song. Such an experience can grow into a project for an entire class.

Older children learn to recognize the inseparability of music and math. Music can become the key to the door behind which fractions have been hiding themselves. The notes in a measure of music must equal the whole—3/4 time requires the value of *three quarter* notes.

And so it goes. Opportunities are all around us.

Rhythm and beat

Rhythm and beat are inseparable. In a marching song, when children clap as they march, the first beat of the 1-2-3-4 time is accented naturally—without even thinking about it. For example:

(4 beats) AN - CHORS A - | WEIGH, MY BOYS |
1- 2   3   4 | 1- 2   3   4 |

In waltz time the first beat again is the one accented 1-2-3.

(3 beats)   SEE | SAW | MARGERY | DAW |
1 - 2 - 3 | 1 - 2 - 3 | 1 - 2 - 3 | 1 - 2 - 3 |

Use whatever is handy

Is there a small drum in the classroom? The teacher drums 1 — 2 — 3 — 4 several times and asks, "What can we do when we hear '1 — 2 — 3 — 4' music? Can we walk? Run? Skip? March?"

Let the children experiment as you repeat the drum beat again and again. They'll soon discover that marching fits four beats perfectly.

You have no drum? Clap your hands, tap with a ruler. (But plan to make a simple drum as part of your science studies. See Chapter 6.)

The children will want to clap, to try the drum, to *accent* (new word?) the first beat.

Still experimenting with four beats, try accenting the first beat (strongly) and the third beat (lightly). 1 2 3 4   1 2 3 4 See

what the class can do to make this slightly different beat more interesting. Let them experiment. One class came up with the idea of using the *drum* for beat *one* and the *triangle* for beat *three*. See what yours can devise.

Use these rhythm ideas

1—"Talk" a song ("My Country 'Tis of Thee"):

$$\frac{3}{4}\; \quad | \quad . \quad | \quad |$$

2—"Talk" and clap a song.
3—Sing and clap a song.
4—Sing and clap as you walk or march to the music of a song.
5—Have a "band" lead the parade. (Good time to use those home-made drums, cymbals and triangles. See Chapter 6.)
6—Choose a drum major with a good sense of rhythm to lead the band that heads the parade.
7—See how the parade perks up when you play the record "Seventy-six Trombones."
8—Follow a similar plan when you and the children experiment with three-quarter time (good rhythm for skating).

Some songs begin on the *last* beat of a measure

When you feel more confident, try the reaction of your class to songs that start on the *last* beat of the measure. You'll be surprised as you look through music books to see how many songs start this way.

For example, in 4/4 time:

```
WE ARE | MAR - CHING  TO  PRE | TOR - IA (rest)
   4   |   1       2    3   4 |   1   2-3    -
```

```
   O | BEAU - TI - FUL  FOR | SPA - CIOUS  SKIES
   4 |   1     2    3    4  |   1      2      3    -
```

Or, in 3/4 time:

```
MY | BON - NIE  LIES | O - VER  THE | O - CEAN |
 3 |   1     2    3  | 1    2    3  | 1   2 - 3 |
```

```
HE | FLIES  THROUGH  THE | AIR  WITH  THE | GREAT  EST  OF | EASE
 3 |   1        2      3  |  1    2    3   |   1     2   3  | 1 - 2 -
```

Never take for granted that your fourth, fifth or sixth grade children have been given sufficient training in rhythm. Try them out first with the simpler methods we have been discussing. You can tell quickly whether or not they're ready for more sophisticated rhythms such as the rumba, tango, bolero, and the syncopation of ragtime. (See Chapter 8.)

A first grade teacher takes a different approach to rhythm

Miss Fanning's first graders had just finished an outdoor game that involved a good deal of running. Now they were back in the classroom enjoying a short rest period.

Tommy came up to his teacher with consternation written all over his little red face.

"Miss Fanning," he said, "feel this," and he stretched out his arm. "Something's beating in my arm. Feel it?"

Miss Fanning felt it. "That's your pulse beating, Tommy. When we run fast our pulse beats fast."

"May I feel your arm?" he asked.

"Yes," answered his teacher, "feel how my pulse beats."

"But it's slower than mine. Why?"

"That's because you were running and I was watching you play. If I had been running my *pulse* would be beating fast, too."

"Feel *my* pulse," demanded Linda.

Tommy thought hers was slower also, but when he tried his own pulse again he found that it had slowed down some.

After Miss Fanning had dutifully felt a dozen or so pulses, she asked if anyone knew a word that means the same as "pulse," and eventually Joanne came up with the word "beat."

"Is there anything in our room that beats like a heart?" the teacher asked.

"The clock on your desk," said Dick, and added, "I can beat time! Watch me, everybody!" And he started to sing and clap his hands to a class favorite:

> "This old man, he played one,
> He played nick-nack on my thumb . . ."

Now the class joined him, clapping hands and singing—

> "With a nick-nack, paddy-whack, give a dog a bone,
> This old man came rolling home."

Tina tried to beat time for "Go Tell Aunt Rhody" but became confused by the slower rhythm of the song.

"It's hard to do this one, Miss Fanning, please help me."

When "Aunt Rhody" had been sung, the teacher asked why Tina had found it hard to *lead her class in singing* (a new term to be used in place of "beat time").

"Because it's slower."

"It's a sad song."

"You can't march to that music."

"It's easier to beat time to fast music."

This first grade was discovering that rhythms vary and you have to beat time (or lead), sing or march to them in different ways.

Soon Miss Fanning will encourage the children to experiment with rhythms using rhythm sticks, a triangle, the classroom drum, and perhaps a small tambourine. (Any of these can be made by teacher and class if the factory-built ones are not available. See Chapter 6.)

The importance of rhythms in your music program

When young children sing, they move without thinking about it—the movement is part of the singing. This may vary from clapping hands or tapping a spoon on a plate to more energetic movements such as skipping, marching or an impromptu dance. But when a child grows up, he is taught to sit still and sing simultaneously, and something natural is lost. Whenever it's possible, and for as long as we can, let's encourage children in our classrooms to fully enjoy music by moving with it.

Rhythms in the classroom

Unfortunately, classrooms seldom have the extra space needed for free movement. By the time you put twenty-five or thirty children, their desks and chairs, and the teacher and her paraphernalia in even a modern schoolroom, not much of the precious space is left for stretching and moving about.

If you have some teaching experience, or even a good memory of your own childhood, you realize that the need to move and stretch is of utmost importance to young animal spirits. When a youngster is physically at ease, he's more manageable—easier to teach.

How can we plan to move as we sing—plan for the rhythms that are food for body and soul? Do all rhythmic movements require room? Can they be enjoyed within the confines of the average classroom?

Let's investigate the possibilities.

The action song

Would it surprise you to learn that "The Little Shoemaker" is still delighting young children? You and I cut our teeth on it and still the song works wonders! Using it as a sample, how many ways can we find to refresh tired little minds and bodies in the limited space of your classroom and mine?

1—*Sing it!* The song is simple, and fun. It will put no strain on your abilities as a performer, so that worry is eliminated. Children love its utter simplicity and find the even, steady beat pleasing and satisfying.

2—*Talk about it!* Everyone has visited the shoemaker's shop. This is a *tiny* one. What tools does the shoemaker use? Would our little man's tools be different? How would you sew a shoe? How would you use a hammer? Let me hear you sing "A rap-a-tap" while you hammer a shoe.

3—*Sing it again!* Show me the wee little man with your thumb and finger. Show me his wee little house by making a steeple of your hands, like this (show them). If a child has another idea for dramatizing parts of the song let him demonstrate.

4—When you and the children get to the *chorus* really sing out on the "rap-a-taps." Relax and enjoy it with the class. Laugh about it. Talk about it. Sing it. Remember how you enjoyed this little song—how many years ago?

5—*Who wants to be in the orchestra?* Now that we are familiar with "The Little Shoemaker," can you think of any way to make the song more fun? Johnny wants to try the rhythm sticks, so he and a friend go off to a corner of the room to practice. Debbie thinks the triangle might sound pretty on the "rap-a-taps," so she will have the opportunity to try her idea. Teacher says she, herself, will experiment with the resonator bells to see if the class thinks they add anything to the production.

You will see how weariness is forgotten in this new interest with its chance to sing, move and plan, and it's only a sample of the magic power of a song—simple though it may be.

"But I can't sing!"

You *do* want to teach rhythm songs (and other kinds, too), but feel you have little singing ability?

1—Try singing along with the children when they're enjoying an old favorite.

2—Encourage the class to sing something they learned in a previous grade—to sing it just for you!

3—Walk around during a song. Listen for the best and truest voices. Plan to use these singers as assistants.

4—Ask one of them to sing something he or she knows. Wouldn't he like to teach it to you and the class?

Some more ideas

1—Suppose you're teaching a second grade. "Borrow" a good singer (recommended by his teacher) from the third or fourth grade. He (or she) will be delighted to help you teach a song learned last year.

2—Use children's records. Music shops have countless fine albums prepared for children. (See Chapter 2).

3—Start with "talking" the record as it plays and proceed to "tapping" it and finally singing along with the record.

4—Ask a more musically gifted colleague to tape a song for you, and use the tape to teach the song. Children find it intriguing and respond enthusiastically.

Some classroom songs for early grades

> *Little White Duck*
> *Peter Cottontail*
> *Three Little Fishies*
> *Sing a Song of Sixpence*
> *She'll Be Comin' Round the Mountain* (try clapping on the off beat)
> *Dickory, Dickory Dock*
> *See-Saw, Margery Daw*

Once the children have learned a song, ask them to suggest motions and instrumentation to add to the enjoyment and enrichment.

The amount of activity possible in any of the above songs is limited only by the space in the classroom. Try walking, hopping, "swimming" up and down aisles and around groups of desks. Your room may even permit the forming of a circle, which always adds to the fun. In a circle you can face partners, clap each others' hands, join hands and walk, march or skip. If the circle must be small, take turns being in the circle or being one of the orchestra in the seats.

Fourth to sixth grades

In these grades children enjoy the rhythmic pattern of a song even more than before. Now they are able to appreciate the delights of syncopation, the rhythmic beat of a pony's hoofs, the p-u-l-l of the anchor, the pounding of spikes into railroad ties. At this age children enjoy the beat of the rumba and conga, and the speed of a good, rousing polka.

All these rhythmic patterns can be tried out by clapping hands, stamping feet—even tapping on one's own desk. As children perfect each rhythm have them investigate classroom instruments. You will find the maracas, tambourine, the old faithful rhythm sticks invaluable. (Several substitutes can be made in school or at home.) Even a rubber ball cut in half makes an effective accompaniment for cowboy songs.

Here are some suggestions for starting your list of rhythm songs for classroom use:

> *I've Been Working on the Railroad*
> *Paddy Works on the Erie*
> *Blow the Man Down*
> *Pull on the Oar, Boys*
> *Goodbye, Old Paint*
> *Daisy, Daisy*
> *Arkansas Traveler*
> *Ferry Me Across the Water*
> *Joshua Fit the Battle of Jericho* (try clapping on the off-
> beat)
> *This Train*
> *Day -o* } Harry Belafonte record suggested for teaching
> *Star -o* } these—RCA Victor 1248 (e) LSP

Ask the children for suggestions for the dramatization of these songs. Here, again, movement need not be restricted to the desk and chair. Study the possibilities your room offers for moving around while singing.

Most of the above songs are to be found in school music books or collections of folk music. The use of the Belafonte record will give your children an introduction to the fascinating calypso beat of the Caribbean Islands.

Rhythms in the gym

Since the gym is available only at specified times, plan to make the best use of it. Now you can take the ideas formed in your classroom and really develop them. The "heave-ho" of the chanty, the "hoppity-hop" down the bunny trail—no matter what your grade may be—this is the time children have plenty of room to move around.

Have your records selected in advance and be sure the record player is in good shape. This is vital to your success in the *classroom*, and you and I know that in the *gym* our control is just a little more difficult to maintain. Let's be prepared.

There are delightful singing and dancing games for all grades. Your physical training syllabus and your music syllabus should have good suggestions. Perhaps your school's music series books have the music for piano and other instruments, plus a detailed description of dance steps. If you're lucky, there may be a record series accompanying the books. In nearly every school there are records available for dancing and marching. If you don't see them around, ask. Many a useful treasure is gathering dust in supply closets—often unopened. But don't despair if the more sophisticated aids are temporarily unavailable. Singing and dancing games are as old as the hills, and you and your class *can* have fun doing just that.

Plan your gym time carefully

In order to save valuable time in the gym—where you may be allotted a mere thirty or forty minutes—teach the words and the music in the classroom. Practice clapping or stamping the rhythm, experiment with suggestions made by the children, become as familiar as possible with the singing game or dance you expect to teach. Your plan for the period may include a rhythm song for which you and the class have worked out some ideas, or it may be a dance you want to try out where there's plenty of room.

Rhythm songs and dances for the gym

EARLY ELEMENTARY GRADES:

The King of France
Bluebird, Bluebird
How Do You Do, My Partner?

*Button, You Must Wander**
*Dance of Greeting**
Pop, Goes the Weasel!

Mulberry Bush   *You Put Your Right*
Foot In
Brother, Come and Dance With Me

FOURTH TO SIXTH GRADES:

Chebogah (Hungarian)
La Cucuracha (Latin-American)
O, Susanna
Sidewalks of New York
The Gypsies Dance*
Carolina in the Morning (create your own dance steps)
Waltz Song (from the German song, "Du, Du")
Song of the Vagabonds (marching, singing, acting)
Hora (Israeli)
Sing and Dance (polka)
La Raspa (Mexican Hat Dance)
Simpler Strauss waltzes (such as "Vienna, City of Song")

Use material available in your school

If you are a new teacher in the school either by appointment or transfer find out what records are available. Inquire in the office or ask someone in charge of music or check with the physical training supervisor. Perhaps there are rhythm instruments you can share with someone on your grade. There may be an unopened set of music readers waiting to be discovered. I know of a school where a new music supervisor unearthed a fine set of never used resonator bells. Every classroom should have its own set, but they're expensive.

Rhythms are wonderful! They're made to order for the person who is timid about teaching music. Not only do they build your confidence and make your children happier, but they can help you as they did Miss Jacobs, in the creative writing of music, reading music, class singing, accompaniments, and part singing.

USE RHYTHMS TO START AN EFFECTIVE
MUSIC PROGRAM

1—Children are born with an innate sense of rhythm, so it is natural to start with rhythms when we introduce children to the joys of music.

---

* H. Wilson, W. Ehret, A. Snyder, E. Hermann, and A. Renna, *Growing With Music* series (Englewood Cliffs, N.J.: Prentice-Hall, Inc., 1966). (Records are available with this series.)

2—As a child advances through the grades he frequently loses his spontaneity—his natural reaction to experiences, musical and otherwise. Beginning *again* with rhythms is the answer.

3—Start with large, simple movements in songs and games. Young children enjoy them more since this fits their stage of development. Older children relax easily with such movements.

4—No matter what the grade, if your class seems reluctant to sing, be alert to any occasion to introduce music to them. Your opportunity may come with a simple game, a math lesson, poetry, or social studies.

5—Rhythm and beat are inseparable. Children enjoy marching and clapping to the 4/4 beat. A small drum adds greatly to the fun.

6—Experiment with children's reaction to: marching rhythms (4/4), waltz rhythm (3/4), songs that start on the *last* beat of a measure.

7—You needn't wait for gym periods to give children a chance to experiment with rhythms. With a little planning, many "action" songs can be enjoyed in the classroom.

8—As children become familiar with "action" songs and games, try using the drum, triangle, maracas, rhythm sticks, and tambourine to add pleasure and enrichment to your music.

9—If your rhythm songs have been tried out in the classroom, you can use the gym period more effectively for marching or skipping as you sing, for circle games, for dances.

10—If you are timid about teaching music, starting with rhythms will build confidence in your ability to teach other kinds of music.

chapter 2

How to Use Singing
in the Classroom

How natural it is for people to sing when they're together! A song sets the mood for a gathering whether it's held in a football stadium or a church. There are songs for any mood and any situation. The folksongs of a nation vary from the patriotic fervor common in wartime to gentle lullabies; from fast-paced dance tunes to tender love songs.

All through history people have sung together. Wouldn't it be too bad if our young generation of TV spectators never learned the delights of joining wholeheartedly in a song—of letting go in joyous singing with their friends? To quote Dr. Oliver Wendell Holmes:

> "Alas for those that never sing,
>   And die with all their music in them!"

There is a grave possibility that some such fate might await today's children unless we teachers do a good job of preventing it.

Years ago parents and grandparents passed on to children the songs of their people. Words and music may have suffered a little in the process but children learned these songs, enjoyed singing with family and friends and passed the songs along to their own babies. A beloved song by Anton Dvořák says, "Now I teach my children each melodious measure."[1] In the rush and tensions of modern life, how often do Mother and Dad take time for such old-fashioned pleasures?

---

[1] From "Songs My Mother Taught Me" by Anton Dvořák.

Get the day off to a good start

When teacher and children meet in the morning they come from homes where the start for the day may have been anything but pleasant. Teachers have their own early dawn problems and children certainly have theirs—even if many such problems are of their own making.

No matter! Meet the class with a smile. It will make you feel better right away. Your children may be surprised, but they'll like it and most of them will respond with a smile, too.

Do you have some kind of opening exercises each morning? It's a good way to smooth the transition from home to school. The period can be short and as formal or informal as you wish, but there should be this time of singing and planning together. It breaks the ice and engenders a feeling of good fellowship, a feeling of belonging to a group.

Some ideas for early elementary grades

1—Begin with a "Good Morning" song. "Good Morning to You" may be a bit shopworn but it's new to little children and they like it. The song is easy to sing but if you're shy about any solo work, join the children and as they sing "Dear teacher," you sing "Dear children."

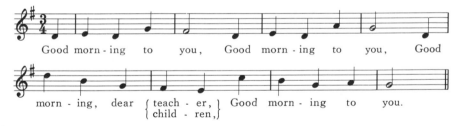

To find your starting note, use a pitch pipe or resonator bells or melody bells. A piano would be ideal but they're rarely found in classrooms. Start the song on "D" (the note above middle C). It may seem low but there's the jump of an octave coming up in the third "Good Morning." Small children do not have much voice range and sing best when high notes are not too high.

2—If it's a child's birthday, bring him to the front with you, put a paper crown on his head and ask the class to sing "Happy Birthday" to him. It's the same tune as "Good Morning."

It is important that you do this for each "birthday child" so look at the birth dates in your records and make note of it when writing your weekly plan.

There will always be a few children whose birthday falls on a week-end or holiday. Plan a little "unbirthday" at the end of the month and have a small group to whom the class sings. Children like a bit of silli-ness once in a while.

3—If it's a famous person's birthday, tell the class a story about him. Show his picture if one is available. Sing "Happy Birthday" to him.

4—Ask the children which of their favorite songs they'd like to sing next. If they don't do well with it, make a mental note to practice it in the near future—but not now. Opening exercises should be free from pressures.

5—Talk over with your class some of the coming activities of the day. There will be math, games, reading, singing, radio or TV pro-grams. Keep a small clothesline across the board and, as you talk and plan with the children, clip cut-out pictures on the line with clothespins —pictures of children playing with alphabet blocks, reading books, singing, playing games, watching TV. This visual program helps them feel they have a part in the smooth operation of the class, gives a sense of belonging to a group, and helps them feel a sense of participation.

By the time children reach second grade there will be some changes in opening exercises. Now they know the words of "America" and the flag salute. Start the day with this more formal beginning and then go on to familiar songs for the repertoire will be more varied.

When the class helps you plan the day, print a list of activities on your blackboard where it can be referred to at any time.

Third grade children are quite capable. There will be some who can help by conducting a song while you walk around and listen to the singing. They may be able to add an innovation or two—under your supervision—to give variety to opening exercises:

    1—try a round instead of a regular song;
    2—have an "orchestra" consisting of two pieces, such as triangle
        and rhythm blocks, to add interest to the music;
    3—just the boys sing this one, the girls the next, blue-eyed
        children another, and brown-eyed people the last.

The Star Spangled Banner—yes or no?

Why Congress ever settled on this song as our national anthem only Heaven knows. (1) It is unsingable—even professional singers are unhappy with it. (2) It's next to impossible to find a good place to take a breath. (3) In spite of years of training, children in junior high school never seem to know the words. (4) Adults certainly don't know them either and (5) are scared to death to sing any part of it except the middle range notes.

Unless your school insists upon the song being part of your opening exercises, you'll be much better off with "America," "America, the Beautiful" or "The Battle Hymn of the Republic." They are simpler and much more musical. The teacher in charge of the assembly music will *have* to teach the "Star Spangled Banner," so let her have the honor—unless you're looking for a number one challenge. At 9 A.M. on a Monday morning—or a Tuesday or a Friday—children and teacher alike are quite incapable of doing it justice.

Opening exercises in fourth to sixth grades

Now your opening exercises can become more meaningful. Try the "leader for the day" plan.[2] This gives each child in your class an opportunity to plan opening exercises on the day that he is leader. *Under his teacher's guidance,* he selects songs to be sung, decides the order of early morning activities such as health inspection and reading the previous day's log, and plans the day with his class.

Each child has a turn—volunteers at first and then those who earlier lacked the courage. This works well because it's something different, gives individuals responsibility, and encourages the development of a good class spirit.

Is there a definite time for classroom singing?

In planning the program of work you have definite periods set aside for each area of study. There are set times when you plan to have a math lesson, reading, social studies, games and, of course, music.

The modern program has become quite flexible and we find that we are teaching math with science, reading as part of social studies—and music? Music fits in everywhere. It, too, must have a definite place in the program, but once we start to think "Music" it's amazing how many times during an average school day music comes to the rescue as a relaxer, a refresher—almost a cure-all for teacher and class.

In Chapter 8 we'll go into detail about the many ways music dovetails with other subjects. But right now we're discussing singing in the classroom—the occasions when children actually sing together. Since

---

[2] Mary Beckwith, *The Effective Elementary School Teacher* (West Nyack, N.Y.: Parker Publishing Company, Inc., 1968).

singing songs means *teaching* songs, let's get right down to the technique that will help you in teaching a variety of songs to your children.

How to teach a new song

There are two ways to teach a new song successfully: 1—by rote; 2—from a record.

1—*By rote:*

> *a*—Choose a simple tune. In early grades a song such as "Go Tell Aunt Rhody"; in third and fourth grades, "She'll Be Comin' Round the Mountain"; for fifth and sixth grades, "Home on the Range."
>
> Each of these songs is in the middle vocal range so a person self-conscious about his voice needn't worry that it might crack on a high note.
>
> Each song is more or less familiar to children and this will make it easier for you to teach it.
>
> Each song has several verses to be enjoyed once the melody has been taught.
>
> *b*—Practice in private or with a sympathetic friend. You *must* know where to start, so learn to use a pitch-pipe since it's small, easy to use, easy to carry with you. (There should be one in your desk. If not, ask for one). Practice giving yourself the proper pitch and finding the starting note. *Become thoroughly familiar with the song.*
>
> *c*—Relax and teach the song informally. If a song develops casually as you talk with the children it's always easier.
>
> *d*—Sing the first verse all the way through, then talk and even laugh with the class about it. Repeat the first line and ask the children to sing it with you—once—twice. Take the second line and follow the same procedure.
>
> Now, you and the class sing both lines together—and so on.
>
> *e*—Altogether, the whole song. Once more for luck.
>
> *f*—Walk around and listen while the class sings it without your help.
>
> *g*—That wasn't so terrifying, was it? Next time around it will be even easier.

Children studying life in Colonial America may enjoy comparing this way of learning a song to the "lining-out" method used in Puritan congregations.

2—Teaching a new song from a record:

Early grades—"The Diesel Train"; third and fourth—
"It's a Hap-Hap-Happy Day"; fifth and sixth—"Tum Balalaika."[3]

> *a*—Select a record where the melody is clearly distinguishable. Some records are confusing for the melody is hidden by sound effects that are unnecessary in classroom use.
>
> *b*—Write the words on the board or project them on a screen.
>
> *c*—Play the record all the way through.
>
> *d*—Talk about it—discuss it.
>
> *e*—Children hum softly as record is played.
>
> *f*—Children sing softly as record is played.
>
> *g*—Try singing without the record. (Proceed slowly with this.)
>
> *h*—Teacher walks around the room while children sing the song (1) *with* the record and (2) without the help of the record. It's easier to notice the weak parts of the song when the class is singing alone.
>
> *i*—When the children are more familiar with the song, discuss with them the possibility of adding some interesting effects of their own, such as a drum beat, rhythm blocks, recorder, tambourine, resonator bells, and so forth. (See Chapter 6.) This idea may be used to advantage in teaching a song *by rote,* also.

As you add more songs to your repertoire

First, we started by singing songs learned in an earlier grade. Then we added a few that are favorites of some of the better singers, plus an occasional contribution by a volunteer from an older class. Now, you are teaching your own songs with and without records and realize you are doing a good job and beginning to enjoy it. It's surprising how quickly the collection grows.

Making use of your song collection

1—As you and your class study a new song, write the name of it on the board (or on a sheet of oak-tag if board space is at a premium). Add the composer's name and some interesting facts about him or the song.

---

[3] All are available from Triton Record Company, 525 Lexington Ave., New York City.

Children from the third year up can add: (1) key in which it is written, (2) starting note, (3) tempo, (4) nation that gave us the song, (5) when it was written, (6) type of song—lullaby? sad? humorous? historic?

For example: "Oh, Susanna!" (Stephen Foster, American composer of folk music 1826–1864)

1—Very popular with '49ers
2—Humorous, sing it brightly
3—Key of F
4—Starting note F
5—Beat 1–2, 1–2

2—On your Music Bulletin Board keep a list of old and new songs the class enjoys. (Some songs just don't "go over" with certain groups. Discard them! There are countless songs all will enjoy.)

3—The "Song Bag" (a grab-bag of songs) is an idea that appeals to children. Use a bag—any kind. It can be as fancy as your class wishes. Keep it in a prominent place.

As a song is learned and perfected and enjoyed, the class secretary prints on a 3″ x 5″ card the name of the song, composer, key, starting note, beat and date on which it was considered worthy of joining the Song Bag collection. Then the card is ceremoniously dropped into *the bag*.

On an occasion when a good song is needed (visiting VIP, assembly contribution, opening exercises, relaxation) pull a card out of the grab-bag, and there you are!

Review these songs from time to time because both you and the children will need a brush-up once in a while.

4—*Tape a song:* This is not only exciting to your class, but the tape points up any weak spots in the music that might otherwise go unnoticed. Have the children make note of such weak spots as they listen to the tape being played back. If there is general agreement that the song should be improved or treated in a different way, practice and re-tape it. Tapes can be played for parents' meetings, for another class or for your own enjoyment.

5—*Interclass visits:* Invite another class on your grade to visit, and entertain the guests with two or three of your favorites. If your visitors would like to learn one of these songs, arrange with the teacher for a return visit for this purpose. Perhaps the other class would like to do the same for you.

6—*Assembly programs:* Use some of your favorites from the Song Bag collection as a foundation for an assembly program put on by your class. Tell the assembly how you plan your Song Bag collection (the children can prepare the script) using two or three songs to illustrate, *or* present short dramatic episodes that tell about the birth of these songs, how a particular song has been used in the past for entertainment or perhaps to celebrate a great event.

Songs that readily lend themselves to such activities:

> The Battle Hymn of the Republic
> Dixie
> Erie Canal
> Go Down, Moses
> I'm a Yankee Doodle Dandy (story of George M. Cohan)

How to improve the quality of the singing

We've been discussing at some length the importance of getting children to sing and to enjoy singing. Now that your children like to sing and look forward to that part of the school day, it's time to think about improving the quality of such singing.

Do you have enthusiastic youngsters with a tendency to shout? Are there others who never have enough breath left to finish a phrase—who breathe in the middle of a word? Is there one who is definitely off pitch and gets hostile looks from those sitting near him? Do you wonder how to get more *feeling* into the songs—gaiety? tenderness? sympathy? spirit? How does Mrs. Jameson get her class to watch her so closely as she directs a song? On the other hand, why can't someone tell Mr. Frank that not all music should be shouted from the housetops, even if his sixth graders seem to like it that way?

Let's look into some of these problems and see if we can find the answers.

Good breathing solves many problems

Even the smallest child can be taught to breathe correctly. You don't *tell* him he's going to learn to breathe deeply—you *show* him. How? The same way you teach so many things in first grade—*make a game of it!* Write your own script—for you know your own class—but follow this plan, always doing everything right along with the children. They will imitate you:

> 1—Stand up and take a B-i-g stretch.
> 2—Hold your arms up high and take a B-i-g breath.
> 3—Hold your breath while we count 1-2-3-4-(slowly).

4—Now, breathe out *slowly* while you bring your arms down.

5—This time take a breath and call softly, "Hel-lo-o-o!"

(Try this with "Good——bye!" "Mom——my!" "Blue—— bird!")

It is important that each step be taken slowly and in a completely relaxed manner. Follow this with volunteers taking the place of the teacher. Then try the same procedure with two words sung on one breath: "Hel-lo Mom-my!" "Good-bye Blue-bird!"

 1 2 3 4 1 2 3 4

When the class becomes familiar with properly combining breathing and singing, take the "Good Morning" song and try singing the phrase "Good morning to you" with just one good breath. Show the children by using your hands expressively when they are to take a breath and how long they are to hold it. (Practice this in front of a mirror until you have the knack of making your hands behave. Tell the children your hands will "talk to them":

"Breathe!"—Extend your arms, palms up, raise palms together, slowly.

"Hold that breath!"—Same position, hands beat 1-2-3-4.

"Breathe out!"—Turn palms down, decisively!

I can guarantee a fascinated audience, but practice in private for perfection —it's well worth the effort.)

Another suggestion for breath control

At another time teach the children to sing a partial scale on one breath:

" Is Tommy here this morning?"
 1 - 1- 2 - 3 - 4 - 5 - 5

And Tommy answers by coming down the scale:

" Yes, I'm here this morning."
 5 4 3 2 1 - 1

Encourage Tommy and all the others on whom you call to take a big, deep breath before answering you. When they get the idea, have them ask each other a variety of questions, but *insist on the breathing part of the game* or it will deteriorate rapidly and be of little benefit.

When your class is older

In the middle and upper elementary grades you will still find poor breathing habits in singing, but with these older children you can take a much more direct approach.

Make this singing lesson part of your health studies:

> 1—Using a chart of the body, explain the position of the diaphragm and its importance in the breathing process.
> 2—Show the children where to place their fingertips on the lower ribs.
> 3—Notice what happens when you take a deep breath.
> 4—Hold that breath and let it out very slowly.
> 5—What happened when you did that?

There may be some giggling, but there will be a great deal of interest in the mechanics of breathing. Tell the children that all good singers learn the importance of deep breathing and that without it even a beautiful voice would be worth little.

You can put this over by having them practice singing whole phrases with *one good breath.*

Use your hands while directing songs to show the class when to breathe and how long to hold the breath. Insist that they watch you carefully. When individual children try leading the class, help them learn how to use their hands the way you do.

It's really a good sign if children start to yawn during singing exercises. They're not sleepy, just relaxed and enjoying themselves.

Overenthusiastic singers

Shouting doesn't improve singing any more than too much amplification improves a band. The singing voice can be soft—or loud—as the occasion demands. It can go high or low, fast or slow, but one never *shouts* a song. Ask your children why each of these statements is true. If they talk it over, it will make a deeper impression.

How can you direct songs so children know when you expect them to sing faster, slower, louder, softer? How can you train overexuberant youngsters to sing music the way its composer intended? Here's the answer: *Plan your music with the same care you give to math or any other subject.*

Do some homework!

There is a definite goal to be realized in each part of the curriculum and, while music is—and should be—less formal, this very fact requires special preparation on your part. To be at ease and less formal in your approach, to be able to enjoy the music with your class, you must have a thorough understanding of the simplest song you plan to teach. *You must be in control of the situation.*

Don't fret about a lack of musical knowledge! Don't feel embarrassed if you have a very average voice! We have emphasized this before and will do it again. These things do not matter to your class. If you can create and hold their interest—that's the most important ingredient needed for a satisfactory music program. To do this you *must* prepare your song, rehearse your manner of directing, study the music reader, practice in private. The same facts hold true even when using a record.

When we discuss later on how to read music from books, you will find that the kind of homework you are doing *now* will stand you in good stead *then*. A foundation will have been laid, and an important part of that foundation is teaching your class to follow your lead—your directing.

If you are teaching by rote a song in the music reader, study the suggestions given for your benefit, such as tempo and expression. Your class will not see the books now because you are teaching this one by rote. When you sing it to them, try to follow any suggestions you find. It gives children the "feel" of the song.

Let's take a concrete example: the old American folk song, "Down in the Valley." Perhaps you have chosen this because it has some connection with a poem being studied, or even with the study of mountain ranges in your social studies, or the *Junior Red Cross Magazine* has a story about mountain people. (It's always more interesting and valuable if it's connected to something else in your daily work.)

As you prepare the song (in private), you notice that the music reader mentions the words "wistful" and "lonesome," and it is to be sung "moderately"—all helpful hints. Don't be frightened by 9/8 time —that's really nothing but a three-part time and this is how it works:

1—9/8 time means there is the value of *nine eighth* notes in each measure.

2—It would be awkward to beat nine times to a measure while directing and difficult for singers to follow.

3—Simply beat three-part time——1—2—3, 1—2—3, 1—2—3.

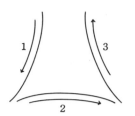

4—"Down in the Valley" begins on the *last* of the measure so "Down in the" is your "3" beat (see illustration), "Val" is the "1" beat and "ley" is the "2" beat.

5—Practice as you hum or sing to yourself and the gentle swing of the three-part time will carry you along with it.

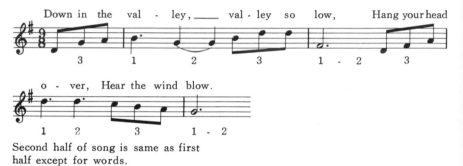

Second half of song is same as first half except for words.

How to use your left hand in conducting

When you watch an orchestra conductor at work, notice how he uses his left hand constantly to get the effects he wants from the musicians in the orchestra. The right hand beats the time and changes the tempo—but see that left hand. Palm is raised—softer. Finger to lips —still too much volume! Palm is clenched—let's have it, boys! When both hands work in unison it means the music has reached a point where the conductor is asking for a special prearranged effect necessary to its perfect rendition.

You can use signals, too. Your children will watch *you* closely and respond to the "Sh—h" sign, the "More volume" sign and—very important—signals for a clean beginning and ending.

Signal for a "clean" beginning:

1—Give class correct pitch. Repeat until satisfied.

2—Extend both arms as for conducting.

3—Remain in this position until every eye is on you.

4—Say softly, "Breathe!"

5—Start to beat the time, counting softly, "1-2-3, 1-2-3, 1-2-3, Sing!" (If the beat is "1-2" or "1-2-3-4" the technique is the same.)

6—Never permit a song to continue if the beginning is not "clean." Repeat immediately.

Signal for a "clean" ending:

1—Most song endings are held for two, three or four beats. Notice carefully how your song is to end. Is it 1-2-3 rest? or 1-2 rest? This is part of your study and preparation.

2—Whatever the ending of a song, do this: on the last count, bring both hands together with a definite twist of the wrists that signifies "STOP!" Take "Down in the Valley" again, for an example. You are beating "1-2-3." On the last word "blow," beat "1," then end cleanly on "2." Why? Because you started the song on the third beat— "Down in the—." Shall we take another example. In "The Battle Hymn of the Republic" you are beating 1-2-3-4. Your last measure is the word "on." Beat 1-2-3 Stop! Why? Because you start on the last beat of a measure with the word "Mine."

Good beginnings and endings require practice both in private and with the children, but perfect starts and endings are well worth the patience.

If you train a class to watch for signals and respond to them, you will find that you hold their attention and interest with this challenge. And what a difference it makes in their singing! The timid singer has more confidence (someone is the boss and tells him what to do); the shouter realizes that now there is something more challenging to be reckoned with; the inattentive child becomes interested.

What to do with the off-pitch singer

Many children who sing off-pitch in the early grades improve without any special training. See that they're seated near singers with clear, true voices, and the difficulty tends to correct itself.

There is at least one in every class who seems completely oblivious to the fact that his voice is not in tune with others. Of course, you wouldn't make fun of him, and it won't help if you say, "Don't sing!" What to do!

1—Without drawing special attention to an off-key singer, be sure to include him in any singing question-and-answer game, such as we use for deep breathing. Never make a point of drilling him—of making him repeat again and again—for there is nothing to be gained by making him self-conscious, and much to be lost.

A teacher friend of mine who loves music but never sings told me that as a child she was not only laughed at by her family but instructed by strict German parents not to spoil the family's singing fun by joining them around the piano. Musically, she always considered herself an outcast. Don't let anything like this happen in your classroom.

2—Play the "Echo" game with your small children, keeping it in the middle range of notes. You call, "Ja-nie," and she answers softly on the same pitch, "Jan-ie." Mix up your calls to good and poor singers so the little ones who *need* the game won't think you're trying to trick them.

3—Puppets are known for their ability to help shy or self-conscious children forget themselves. Often a boy or girl wearing the simplest kind of paper-bag disguise can forget himself and take part in the dramatization of a nursery rhyme or song.

4—Encourage poor singers to accompany others with a drum, a triangle or some other instrument that permits them to feel they have an important part in any musical program.

Most off-pitch singers improve gradually. It may be a lack of maturity in some; in others, a lack of interest. Be patient and uncritical of them. See that they're included when you have singing games. Put them near good singers whenever possible.

New and old favorites of children

Some of the songs you teach your class are favorites of parents and even grandparents. How delighted is the child who brings home a song new to him and finds that Grandma learned it in her school and still remembers it well.

When I was a child in school we learned what my teacher laughingly called a "nonsense" song, and I ran all the way home to sing it for my folks. As I started "Ke-mo Ki-mo, dee ro art . . ." my father joined me and we sang together, "me-he me-hi, me hum-drum penny winkle, Tit, tat, pitty-pat, blue-eyed pussy cat, Sing song Kitty can't you Ki-me-o?"

Mother seemed to think it was pretty silly, but she joined the fun and was as thrilled as I to hear that "Papa" had learned it in *college!*

Make the singing of songs so enjoyable to the children in your class that they will want to share the pleasure with others. Many of these songs will become a part of their lives, and perhaps they will pass on to other generations the gift you have made to them.

Here is a list of twenty-four songs—some old, some fairly new—

that I find are favorites of the many children with whom I have sung them. There are a few suitable for nearly any grade, and others definitely for smaller children.

You will, of course, have many of your own to add. Keep it as a working reference list—and have fun with them!

Twenty-four favorites—old and new—for classroom singing:

Early Elementary:
1—Ten Little Indians
2—Jimmy Crack Corn*
3—Go Tell Aunt Rhody*
4—Pufferbillies
5—Jingle Bells*
6—Little White Duck
7—Peter Cottontail
8—Michael Finnegan*

Third and Fourth Grades:
9—Daisy, Daisy
10—In the Good Old Summertime
11—Down in the Valley
12—Yankee Doodle
13—Sidewalks of New York
14—This Train
15—It's a Hap-Hap-Happy Day

Upper Elementary:
16—Shenandoah
17—Blow the Man Down
18—Poor Wayfarin' Stranger
19—Battle Hymn of the Republic
20—Sweet Betsy from Pike
21—Song of the Vagabonds
22—Erie Canal
23—Kum Ba Yah
24—You're a Grand Old Flag

HELPING TODAY'S CHILDREN DISCOVER THE JOY OF SINGING TOGETHER

1—The joy of singing together may be lost to this generation of TV spectators unless teachers do something about it.

2—Some kind of opening exercises helps to smooth the transition

---

* Older children enjoy these too.

from home to school. Singing familiar songs breaks the ice and gets the day off to a good start.

3—There are two good ways to teach a new song: (*a*) by rote, and (*b*) using a record.

4—In either case, be sure you are familiar with the song so you can relax with the children as you teach it.

5—When the class repertoire of songs begins to grow, plan to use the songs frequently. To help you do this:

a—Keep a class record of each song—type, composer, beat, starting note, a fact or two.

b—Keep a music bulletin board where new songs are listed.

c—Keep a "Song Bag" collection of favorites that can be used at a moment's notice.

d—"Tape" some class favorites.

e—Plan an assembly program using class favorites.

6—It is important that children learn to breathe deeply as they sing. This can be taught in lower grades by making a game of it. Older children can be given a more direct approach.

7—The teacher *must practice* conducting songs and train the class to watch for his signals that add so much to the singing.

8—Off-pitch singers are often helped by, (*a*) sitting near children with clear, true voices, (*b*) "Echo" games, (*c*) acting out the part of a puppet, (*d*) accompanying other singers with some instrument such as a small drum or a triangle. The last two devices instill confidence in a timid child.

9—Your children will love to sing if you relax and sing with them. They will not be critical of your voice nor of small mistakes if you and they learn to love music together.

chapter 3

Helping Children
to Appreciate Music

It is through listening that we become familiar with the world of music. From the time a child is born he is surrounded by the sound of music. In the crib there are musical animals to play with, musical lamps to amuse him. Sounds of radio and TV permeate his waking and sleeping hours and the home may enjoy the dubious luxury of taped music in every room. Mother takes him on a shopping trip and music follows him as he is wheeled around in a supermarket cart. It seems there's no escape.

We hear a variety of opinions about the effect of the constant assault of music on the modern child. Some who have studied the problem say, "Wonderful! Children are gaining a cosmopolitan taste in music. They will choose what they like and ignore the rest." But other critics, just as qualified, fear the constant bombardment may cause a child to erect a protective wall against music in much the same way as he tries to protect himself from the sound of a nagging voice.

This is a problem we have to face. The air is filled with music and it's going to stay that way. Much of it is trivial and soon dies from overexposure. Some of it is fine, pleasing to the ear and we want children to be able to enjoy it.

Let's not hurry to join the ranks of those who think no good music has been written since the year 1920. There is a great deal of excellent music, both modern and time-tested, coming over the air and available on records. There is a tremendous variety which includes classics, popular music from shows, jazz, blues, swing, singing groups (a few of which are good). Even atonal music has its fans who insist that to understand is to love.

Most children *like* music. In spite of the fact that they are surrounded by it they want their own record players, their own albums, their own transistor radios. Teachers know that, given some incentive, children like to sing, too. The logical solution is *intelligent guidance* so children may learn to be more discriminating in the music they choose.

It doesn't mean that we want to raise a generation of music snobs. Ideally, youngsters who have all types of music available at the turn of a dial can *learn* to enjoy a little of everything, and by training the ear will learn to appreciate the fine points of mood, tone, melody, harmony and rhythm. They will be able to separate the good from the sensational. This is where the teacher comes into the picture, one who may not be talented but likes music and wants to do the best he can for the children in his class.

Background music

"Background music!" you may say, "isn't that what children are surrounded by all the time?"

Perhaps, but good background music doesn't "surround" anyone, nor should it intrude. It is used ". . . as an accompaniment to some activity essentially unrelated to it . . ." to quote from the dictionary. Can background music help us in the classroom?

That is the question Mr. Landers asked himself. His fifth graders seemed to have little interest in music. Mr. Landers felt he might be at fault for he was inexperienced at teaching, and although he was doing fairly well in some fields the results in music were disheartening.

Facing the problem

One evening Mr. Landers sat down with a pad and pencil. He had decided to face this music problem of his in the most practical way he knew, and would start by listing in black and white anything that was pertinent to it:

1—I'm a graduate of the state college for teachers.

2—No classroom experience in teaching music; observed three

music lessons last year in training.

3—I am literally *crazy* about music, guess I'm a buff.

4—But I play no instrument, can't sing much—just a spectator.

5—I would like to help these children love music the way I do.

6—My taste runs from Bach to Dixieland.

7—How can that help me when I pass out the music readers? That was a disaster!

8—The children don't sing even in assemblies unless I glare at them.

9—I dread the first part of the morning.

10—How does a teacher get a class moving?

His room at home was filled with the rich tones of a cello playing Bach's "Arioso." Good old record player! How faithfully it presented his private concert each evening. Some concert! A little Bach, a little Beatles, something from Broadway (tonight it was "Maria" from Bernstein's "West Side Story"), and often there would be a record by a Dixieland band he had heard perform in New Orleans. Pretty unorthodox taste, but he liked it. Wouldn't Mrs. Carpenter be surprised? She had been so kind to him, a young, green teacher, helping him with advice about the everyday problems of planbooks, duties, parents— giving him time that her own class needed. But when it came to teaching music she just laughed and said, "Oh, you'll learn. It takes time. We all had the same trouble." Come to think of it, he heard very little music wafting across the hall from Mrs. Carpenter's room.

"Well, back to my own problem. I'm trying to teach music to these kids the way it was taught to me in school. We 'do—mi—soled,' tapped the time on our books—it was awful. How I hated music periods! Never did like music until Mom gave me a record player when I was in junior high. Then I began buying my own records."

Records! No, that wasn't the whole answer. Children heard records and bought records all the time these days. Maybe if he played it cool, didn't talk about it, just a record, carefully chosen, played at the right time—what could he lose?

Young, inexperienced, practical, music-loving Mr. Landers did some homework that evening—music homework. He spot-checked his albums, selecting each record with much thought, making notes as he worked. There was Handel's "Water Music," a good straightforward rendition of "America, the Beautiful," "March from the River Kwai," "Home on the Range," Strauss' "Tales from the Vienna Woods," Chopin's "Etude in E major," which became the theme for a popular song.

"There's variety enough for any occasion," he said to himself, "but I'll take along the 'Sound of Music' album and a couple of Liszt's 'Hungarian Rhapsodies.' Even those kids of mine can't resist Gypsy tunes."

Just in case the classroom record player was in a contrary mood, or hadn't been returned by the last teacher who borrowed it, Mr. Landers put his own "old faithful" in the car to be ready for work in the morning.

Putting background music to work

Mr. Landers arrived at his school twenty minutes earlier than usual to set the stage for his experiment. When the class appeared at the door he stepped into the hall, said nothing, just held up a hand until all was calm. Still without a word he leaned toward the open door of the room as though trying to hear something inside. Children are always curious about the actions of a person who says nothing but obviously knows something interesting. They listened, too. There were the soft notes of a melody that one could not quite catch out in the hall. Mr. Landers signalled the first few in line to enter the room.

He stood in the doorway where he could watch what was going on. Soon the children had put away coats and sweaters and had gone to their seats with nothing more than one or two hand signals from the teacher. Not a word had been spoken. No explanation, no attempts at questions encouraged. Just Handel's "Water Music" filling the quiet room with its charm.

When the music ended Mr. Landers greeted his class—still no explanations—and handed the flag to the class president for a morning salute.

Then he started the record of "America, the Beautiful"[1] that he had brought from home. A voice here and there tentatively joined in, and before long the class was singing—his class singing! And he hadn't glared at them once.

Deciding not to push his luck, Mr. Landers went on with the regular morning routines. When he had a moment he put "March from the River Kwai" on the turntable to have it ready for the next experiment. When it was time for the children to leave their room and take the long walk to the gym—something that was often a minor disaster—the young teacher started the record. Mentally crossing his fingers, he

---

[1] I suggest this record: Victor LSP 2687—U.S. Marine Band presents several lively marches and two patriotic songs (no words). First stanza of "America, the Beautiful," offers fine accompaniment for children's voices.

went to the board and wrote, "Girls, on line for gym," and then "Boys, on line for gym." They didn't quite march to the music while getting on line, but they were intrigued and consequently forgot to push and shove.

Leaving the dependable class secretary, Linda, to shut off the record player, Mr. Landers followed his class down the hall. He smiled to himself as he heard a few softly whistled measures of "March from the River Kwai."

Mr. Landers is off to a good start. He has succeeded in getting the class to sing voluntarily and to listen quietly. He has aroused their curiosity. They have begun to respond.

The battle is far from won, but the teacher feels he has a workable plan. It will require a good deal of thought to carry out the campaign, but he is willing to do the necessary homework—and this kind of homework is dear to Mr. Landers' heart.

He expects that the children's natural curiosity will be working for him. When they ask about the music he will talk about it, and he has much to tell them.

Other ways to use background music

1—Teachers of early grades find background music encourages little children to enjoy a quiet rest period. It isn't necessary to play something they know—in fact, many teachers believe there is more relaxation to be found in a selection unfamiliar to the class. They drink their milk, or put heads down for forty winks while some pleasing music is playing softly. If a child wants to know what it is, just tell him, and make no other comment.

2—Children of all ages like to draw and paint to the sounds of background music. These are the times when a child paints whatever he wishes. If the music inspires him to paint a certain picture, fine! Usually the music is a quiet, comfortable setting for his experience with paints or crayons and relaxes rather than inspires.

3—Try using background music to smooth over some of the awkward periods we all meet now and then. With one group it may be the beginning of the morning, but with another class it could be the times they come back from assemblies or gym—or things may reach a low ebb in your room when books and other material are being passed out and collected.

Experiment with various types of music (see p. 56). "Fun" music isn't a good idea for a background at any time. Neither is a record that features a speaking voice. Each of these demands some active response from the children, which is fine—at some other time.

4—You will find making your own tape recording of background music very satisfying. You can record on tape music you have found works well, you will be familiar with it, and you will avoid the confusion that results from not having the right record at your fingertips at the moment you need it.

You may find, also, that some of the following suggestions for background music can become very "active" as the children's interest is aroused. Good! Just switch them from your background collection to your active list.

Here are some ideas for records (or for those private tapes) that can prove very worthwhile in your experiments. This is merely a start, for you will add to it frequently:

Records for background music

Bach, Johann Sebastian—(Stokowski recording) Fugue in G minor (The Little Fugue)	Capitol	SP8484
Beethoven—Sonata #14 in C sharp (Moonlight)	London	6188
Berlioz—Harold in Italy, (Wm. Primrose viola)	Columbia	ML4542
Chopin—24 Preludes (Artur Rubinstein piano)	Victor	LM1163
Dvořák—New World Symphony (#9 in E)	Columbia	ML5793
Enesco—Roumanian Rhapsody #1	Capitol	SP8680
Gershwin—Rhapsody in Blue	Columbia	CL700
Grieg—Piano Concerto in A	Angel	35561
Grofé—Grand Canyon Suite	Columbia	ML6018
Handel—Water Music	Columbia	ML5417
Haydn—Symphony #94 in G ("Surprise")	Victor	LM2394
MacDowell—Woodland Sketches	Vanguard	1011
Mendelssohn—Midsummer Night's Dream	Columbia	ML6028
Mozart—Homage to	Decca	DL9833
Ravel—Bolero	Columbia	CL1898
Schubert—8th Symphony (Unfinished)	Victor	LM2516
Schumann—Carnaval	Columbia	ML4772

Sibelius—Finlandia	Victor	LM1752
Tchaikovsky—Waltzes from Nut-	Columbia	MS7133
cracker Suite and Sleeping Beauty		

There will be many more recordings—perhaps favorites of yours, and not necessarily classics—that you will prefer using. Just be sure you review them beforehand so you know this is the music needed for the occasion. Be familiar with the records, mono or stereo, and with the record player to be used. Usually "ML" or "LM" means "mono," and "S" means "stereo." Since not all record players play both types of records, be careful to check well ahead of time.

See what your school music library has to offer, for there may be some fine recordings there. Be prepared to bring an occasional record from your own collection. Keep a list of records for the school to buy when funds are available.

One excellent bargain is "The Treasury of the World's Most Honored Musical Favorites"—more than 150 selections of classic and popular music made available by The Longines Symphonette.[2] Many of these are ideal for background music and others are better for guided listening. Each is played by the orchestra—there is no vocal music—the numbers are varied, and none is long.

The Longines Symphonette sends the collection on approval, so you have an opportunity to try it out before deciding to buy it.

There is another "Treasury" somewhat similar to this which is a "Sing-a-long" for classroom fun. It features the "Choraliers" accompanied by The Longines Symphonette.

"An Autochthonous Approach"

Not too long ago I saw a booklet advertised by the Music Educators National Conference. It is called "An Autochthonous Approach to Music Appreciation"[3] and is reprinted from the *Music Educators Journal*. The word "autochthonous" attracted my attention and I sent for the booklet—just a few pages long, but it's a gem! Katherine Scott Taylor tells a gentle, satisfying story of her experiences with music while trying to work with a pitifully deprived group of twenty-five first graders from a migrant camp.

This fine, understanding teacher considered herself inexperienced

---

[2] "The Treasury of the World's Most Honored Musical Favorites"—The Longines Symphonette Society, Symphonette Square, Larchmont, N.Y. 10538.
[3] Katherine Scott Taylor, *An Autochthonous Approach to Music Appreciation*, Music Educators National Conference, 1201 Sixteenth St., NW, Washington, D.C. 20036 $.25.

but the story of how she brought something good into those sad little lives should be required reading for all of us. She used background music for rest periods, for learning to write, for lunch times. The records, brought from the teacher's home collection, would be considered way beyond the understanding of a small child—Bach, Beethoven, Mozart—but the miracle took place. No music was ever forced upon the children—it was *they* who sought the meaning of it.

There came a time when some of these little ones began to respond more actively to certain records—humming a theme from one, dancing to another, comparing the rhythms of the selections they heard. None of the records used would ordinarily be thought suitable for such young children, but one boy said, "That makes me want to laugh," and teacher and child laughed together. Another inquired, "What kind of a thing makes that noise?" and was shown a picture of a man playing a cello. Tensions lessened and learning became possible.

Guided listening

We have been discussing the important role of background music in your classroom. Even though such music is unrelated to the activity going on at that time, your opportunity to guide the children musically may develop from one of these selections. It will be one that has attracted the attention of the class—caught their fancy—their interest. This enables you to use the interest in a song or orchestral number to teach something new about music.

Your opportunity may come when the children are attracted by the rhythm or beat of what they are hearing—or when it is the mood of the selection that impresses them. It may be that the music sounds like something familiar—or even its totally different style could be the appeal.

Be alert to such opportunities. This is particularly important if you have found your children generally uninterested in music, for now's your chance—the one you've been hoping for. They will accept something new in music when their interest is roused by their own curiosity. Now you can begin to guide a class—gently and cautiously at first, using your sense of timing, never forcing a situation lest they back away. The interest in music builds, one stone on another, and what you and your class build here will last all their lives.

It's easier when a class comes to you with a normal love of music, or when the school has a well-planned program followed through the grades. But who ever said we became teachers because we wanted an easy job? Teaching is one challenge after another, and it doesn't take long to find how true this is of music.

A listening experience in early grades

As we said in Chapter 2, *singing* is pretty well taken care of in first and second grades because little children have learned to sing with their kindergarten teacher and the interest in it carries over and helps greatly in the next grade or two. You may find that the very same children who like to sing and sing may be quite inattentive when you want them to enjoy *listening,* for *listening* doesn't just happen; it must be taught.

Since we realize that the smart way to teach anything is to connect it with something the children already know, let's plan to do just that. Instead of treating singing and listening as two separate, distinct lessons for our smaller pupils, plan to sing *and* listen while enjoying a song. Let's take "Pufferbillies,"[4] for example—a song with rhythm, action, a good melody, and the appeal that machinery has for children:

1—Show pictures of pufferbillies (steam engines).

2—Talk about pufferbillies. How do they run? Who drives them? What kind of noise do they make? Let's make a noise like a pufferbilly. What causes this sound? Do pufferbillies make another kind of noise? Let's try that, too.

3—Read "The Little Engine That Could" to your class; children still love that little engine. "Can you 'talk' like the little engine?"

4—Select some children to pretend they're a little engine with its cars. The class sings "Pufferbillies" as the "train" departs on its journey around the room.

5—The class discovers that the music must be loud and clear when the train is near them, and gradually diminish as the train is farther away.

6—As they begin to *listen* they discover that music is faster or slower, louder or softer, happy or sad.

Another listening experience

Now let's see what happens as you and the class turn to the study of the melody. (We're still working on "Pufferbillies" for our illustra-

---

[4] H. Wilson, W. Ehret, A. Snyder, E. Hermann, and A. Renna, *Growing With Music—Book I* (Englewood Cliffs, N.J.: Prentice-Hall, Inc., 1966).

tion, but you can try the following on a variety of songs in any grade):

1—After the children are familiar with the song tell them to listen very carefully while you (the teacher) sing it to them, for you are going to ask an important question. (If you prefer, the children can sing it with you.)

2—"Did anyone notice whether or not we sang the first part of the music more than once?" (Hum it over again.)

3—They will discover that lines one and three are the same; that line two is different, and so is line four.

4—"Why do you suppose a song is written this way?" ("It sounds nice"—"I like it that way"—"I like a change in the music"—"I like to hear the first line again.")

You are teaching the children to recognize the "form" of a song. There is a beginning, a middle, an ending; there is repetition in music. This *does* make music interesting; this *is* pleasant to the ear—as they observed. Help them watch for this in songs and recordings. Teach them how to *listen,* for careful listening is the foundation on which we build musical experiences.

There will be many more musical experiences for your children in the early grades that vary from distinguishing between *music* and *noise* all the way to the recognition of simple harmony. Be sure that your class hears many types of recordings; sings many types of songs; has the privilege of playing simple classroom instruments; hears the live music—or the recordings—of the more familiar instruments, such as the piano, organ and violin, and starts to learn about bands and orchestras. Now is the time to encourage courteous "audience" listening.

Children six to eight years old are very much interested in their immediate world: people in the home, pets, beds, chairs, tables, food— this is what they like to talk and sing about. The milkman, the postman, the garbage truck, the bus that passes the house or apartment building—all these are very much a part of the young school-child's world. He starts with such everyday things as the topics of his conversation, questions and songs, and gradually enlarges his horizon.

Middle graders are more perceptive listeners

A child becomes more discriminating as he listens to music—becomes aware that he enjoys some songs and recordings more than others. Perhaps he even asks himself—or his teacher—why this is so. (He is learning that, for one reason or another, not all the music he hears is pleasant and enjoyable.) Here is our opportunity to experiment with the more complex forms of musical enjoyment—the harmony of voices in the classroom, an accompanying instrument playing a third higher or lower than the voices, a recording of a violin and piano duet. We have the world of music at our fingertips, and can give children an ever increasing variety to match and further their growing awareness.

Learning about the orchestra

Interest in the orchestra builds up very gradually. Here again we start with what a child knows—the simple classroom instruments used to accompany him as he sings, marches or dances. There is some natural curiosity about what makes the instrument "tick"—why a person uses breath to make one kind work, and a stick for another.

If the children have had any experience making their own instruments (see Chapter 6), they are quite curious about the workings of the more elaborate models used in orchestras and bands. If they have experimented with the actual making of one, or just played resonator bells, a little drum or a recorder in the classroom, their interest in musical instruments has started to take root and the teacher goes on from there.

Records are available that explain how each of the more popular band and orchestral instruments is used and how it sounds. It is most important to have large, clear pictures that show the instruments, how each is held, and what else the player needs to produce tones; for example, a bow, hammer or drumstick.

Ideally, children should have the opportunity of *seeing* a person in the act of *playing* the instrument. The presence of the performer is best for he can answer questions and let the listeners *feel* the violin—or perhaps the clarinet—what it's made of, how many keys there are—and why; what those curious pegs are doing on the violin—and only *four* strings!

It would be fine to arrange for the visit of an accomplished artist, either in your classroom or the assembly hall. The next-best treat would be a film or a TV program. Your class might be thrilled if a child from sixth grade—one who has passed the beginner stage—brought his guitar, trumpet, clarinet or violin into your room and showed everyone what it was all about.

One of our teachers who had played the violin rather well some years earlier practiced at home and got up enough courage to give her sixth graders a lesson in the workings of the instrument. Needless to say, the youngsters were delighted and had the opportunity of look-ing, listening, touching the violin and asking questions. A firsthand experience such as this means a great deal.

How to "teach the orchestra" to your class

There is more than one way to explain the orchestra to your group, but I have found that studying the individual instruments—their ap-pearance and tone, and *listening under the guidance of the teacher* to recordings of one instrument at a time gives a better understanding of the orchestra.

When children have become familiar with a stringed instrument, such as the violin, they enjoy meeting its cousins, the viola, cello, and the fascinating double (or contra) bass. Have some good pictures of the string family so your class knows not only what each looks like—how they are similar or different—but how the player holds each.

Be sure the children have the best listening experience possible as part of their appreciation of the family of strings. Choose a recording that features one instrument at a time, such as Schubert's "Ave Maria" for the violin; one movement of Berlioz' "Harold in Italy," featuring the viola; or Saint-Saën's "The Swan," which is a favorite cello solo. Avoid playing a long recording of *anything,* for children get enough very quickly.

Talk about your record before playing it, and let them talk too. Establish an air of pleasant anticipation. Make sure the classroom is well ventilated and the children are comfortable. (These necessary precautions are frequently overlooked and teachers wonder why a les-son falls flat.)

You needn't talk about the composer at this point—unless there's a definite interest shown in him. Concentrate on the instrument first and the composer will get his innings in due time.

That interesting bass fiddle

Children love to talk about the double bass. Nowadays its principal role seems to be found in pounding out the rhythm. (Some child whose parent or older brother is a jazz buff may surprise you with the ex-pression "pounding the dog-house.") When we discuss jazz in a later chapter we'll go into detail about the place this huge fiddle holds in the hearts of its devotees.

Since the double bass is rarely used as a solo instrument it would be better to emphasize its importance as the foundation of a string quartet, or a quintet such as Schubert's famous "Trout" Quintet[5] for piano, violin, viola, cello and double bass. Its fourth movement, "Theme and Variations," is ideal for children because it takes one of Schubert's early songs, "The Trout," and repeats its delightful melody over and over in the variations. In this movement the double bass is quite pronounced as a foundation for the other instruments and at times has a little melody of its own.

Here is an instrument that leads a double life and your class will enjoy the idea that the double bass can be the soul of dignity in classical music and can be just as easily "slapped" by the player in a jazz band to emphasize the beat with a kind of heavy-handed humor.[6]

The String Orchestra

The violin and its cousins are so well liked by the great majority of people that orchestras featuring strings are very popular. One of the better known orchestras of this kind is that of Annunzio Mantovani[7] who is noted for his "cascading strings." After your children have made the acquaintance of the violin family, let them hear "Stardust," "Moon River," "Hello Dolly," or almost any one of Mantovani's arrangements of popular and semi-classical selections featuring the close harmonies of the strings.

The haunting tones of the woodwinds

Here is a family whose members have little in common with each other save for the fact that each is basically a tube, with holes, that encloses a column of air. From there on each woodwind differs much in sound and, to some extent, in the way one plays it.

The most familiar are the flute, clarinet, oboe and saxophone, but, like human families, they have relatives. The fife, piccolo and recorder are related to the flutes. Clarinets come in B-flat, A, E-flat and bass, each having its own place of importance in the orchestra. The mellow but melancholy oboe is first cousin to the bassoon and the English horn. Saxophone family members come in *sopranino* (new word?) soprano, alto, tenor, baritone and bass.

---

5 "Trout" Quintet—Schubert—Columbia ML 6467.
6 "A Night at Dixieland Hall," Albert (Papa) French and his New Orleans Jazz Band with Stuart Davis on the bass.
7 Mantovani, "Sentimental Strings," The Longines Symphonette Society, Symphonette Square, Larchmont, N.Y. 10538.

Just as we put our stringed instruments together and listened to their harmonies in a quintet and an orchestra of strings, we can guide a class in the understanding and recognition of woodwinds by selecting a composition featuring these instruments.

I know of nothing more appropriate or more entertaining to children than Prokofiev's "Peter and the Wolf." Each of the woodwinds introduces one of the characters in the story and it isn't very long before your children are able to recognize flute, piccolo or bassoon.

There is a recording available that features two completely appropriate and entertaining selections. One is "Peter and the Wolf" and the other is Benjamin Britten's "Young Person's Guide to the Orchestra." The first features woodwinds; the second takes the orchestra as a whole and then proceeds to explain the importance of each of the instruments. Having two such fine selections on one record is a wonderful idea—and also a good investment (Eugene Ormandy and the Philadelphia Orchestra—Columbia ML 5183 or MS 6027).

The exciting brass

No other music creates quite the same response in human beings of all ages as that of the brass band. Spectators watching a parade simply cannot keep hands or feet from beating time. Even the policeman's horse catches the spirit of the music and comes down the avenue on dancing feet. Flags flying, drum majors and majorettes in colorful costumes—all lend themselves to the exciting spectacle. And the brass! Augmented by plenty of woodwinds and percussion. Is it any wonder that children forgetting parental warnings, follow too far and get lost?

These same brass instruments—trumpets, trombones, tubas—are just as much at home in a symphony orchestra, a dance band or a jazz band, as they are in a parade. The trumpet is penetrating and brilliant, or soft and coaxing—as musician and score demand; a slide trombone, in the right hands, seems almost able to talk; the tuba, like other basses in strings and woodwinds, acts as a foundation and accents the beat.

Use popular music, too

Teachers sometimes hesitate to use any records that are not considered "classical" in presenting instrumental music to a class. This would be a mistake for several reasons:

1—If you use the principle of *starting with something the children know* you will often start with popular music.

2—There is a wealth of good popular music, and the records are easily available and comparatively inexpensive.

3—Popular music is more readily accepted by nearly everyone, for there is a tendency to shy away from something that might be described vaguely as "high-brow."

4—As your class grows in its understanding of music it will accept the classical and listen intelligently *under your guidance.*

5—It would be unrealistic to ignore the appeal of popular music.

You may use a classical recording to illustrate *one* point you want to make, and on another occasion popular music is obviously more suitable. In the study of an instrument don't hesitate to let the children hear both classical and popular, for this points up the versatility of, for example, a trumpet, or a bass fiddle.

For illustrating the trumpet to younger children there is Scott's "The Toy Trumpet" and also "Parade of the Wooden Soldiers." But when you come to fourth, fifth and sixth grades be sure to let these youngsters hear the perfect contrast of Herb Alpert with his Tijuana Brass[8] and Armando Ghitalla playing *any* movement of Hummel's "Concerto in E" with the Boston Chamber Ensemble under the baton of the late Pierre Monteux.[9] Here you have the trumpet skillfully played by masters of "pops" and of the classical.

While we're talking about trumpets we must include Louis Armstrong, "Satchmo," "The King," who celebrated his golden anniversary in show business in October, 1965. This good-will ambassador has traveled over Europe and other parts of the world carrying American jazz to excited audiences in every city.

Almost any trumpet solo of Louis Armstrong's is a treat, so take your choice. If there is a TV show coming up with "Satchmo" as guest artist be sure to urge your children to watch him and listen to him when the opportunity comes. He is one of the "greats."

Ask the proprietor of your music store for a recent issue of "Schwann's Record Catalog"—it's free—and you will find anything you can imagine in recordings listed there. This will be a great help to you as you plan a program of intelligently guided listening for the class. Whether it's new or old, pops or classical, if the record has not been discontinued it will be listed. I have found people in music stores

8 "Whipped Cream," Tijuana Brass, A and M Records—LP 110.
9 "Concerto in E," Hummel, Armando Ghitalla and Boston Chamber Ensemble, Cambridge—(1) 819.

very helpful in suggesting records that can be used to demonstrate and explain musical problems for teacher and class. If you have the opportunity to suggest how some of the school allowance is to be spent, "Schwann's Record Catalog" and your music store proprietor can offer many worthwhile suggestions.

Introducing the composers

When children who like music reach fourth grade they tend to become curious about who *wrote* the music. Nine-year-olds have left behind the interest in things in their immediate surroundings such as garbage trucks and tables and chairs. Now their world expands to include people they have never seen, cities and countries they have never visited. These children are ready to "meet the composers."

Let it happen, if you can. Perhaps Billy, who is studying the piano, tells you he has a new piece, a sonatina by Beethoven. He's very proud and wants to tell the class about it. Encourage him to talk. As he tells of his triumph the children will ask him questions and one of them is sure to be, "What name did you say?" It may be that no one is familiar with the giant, Beethoven. Resist the temptation to tell a long story of a frowning, shaggy-haired man. Start by telling your class that little Ludwig's father liked to boast about his son who at *nine years of age* played very, very well on the piano. The proud father would come home late at night with a few friends, drag the sleepy child from bed and seat him at the piano to entertain his guests.

Now your class has a feeling of sympathy for this child—their interest has been wakened—they are ready for more. Perhaps you can play a recording of a Beethoven sonatina, such as the record available from Baroque Records 1849 which features two sonatinas (little sonatas). The children will enjoy listening to the great composer's "Moonlight Sonata" (London—6188). Tell the class that Beethoven wrote the song they are going to hear. Don't name it—yet. Play the first movement—it's not too long, and very lovely—and ask your audience what the music is trying to tell them. You'll be surprised how close they can come to the mood of the composer.

When Billy has had plenty of time to practice, ask him if he would like to play "his" sonatina for the class on the auditorium piano. Then you will have three or four Beethoven selections to start your notebook and bulletin board lists of composers and their works. A committee of four good readers can gather more information about Ludwig van Beethoven to share with the rest.

Another possibility

Your class has been enjoying "O, Susanna!" They've sung it often and even made up their own dance steps to it. Suppose you surprise them sometime and ask—out of a clear sky—"Who wrote 'O, Susanna!'?" Maybe they'll surprise *you* by knowing the answer and you can find out how much they already know about Stephen Foster, the composer of some of our country's most familiar songs. Fair warning! Don't *you* be surprised if, in this age of TV groaners and shouters, your ten- and eleven-year-olds never heard of the man! It's time they did.

Combine the old and the new

Your music syllabus suggests records to be played throughout the various grades. If you're lucky enough to have an up-to-date music syllabus there will be *more* than classics and semi-classics on the list. But as a rule such lists are pretty conservative and you'll have to look long for anyone who's a product of Broadway, such as George M. Cohan, Irving Berlin or Rodgers and Hammerstein. When we realize how much genuine pleasure these gentlemen have given us it seems they surely deserve a place in our private Hall of Fame.

In a later chapter we'll see how two teachers in different situations guided their classes in the study of music and composers. Both classes shared their information with others in the school—one presenting a program of classics, and the other, Broadway.

Music appreciation

The term "Music Appreciation" may elicit a shudder from one person and a feeling of pleasant warmth in another. The appreciation of music cannot be forced on anyone, for appreciation of music, art, or literature, or a friend, means understanding, and understanding is a gradual process.

In years past too much school music consisted of mechanical singing of prescribed songs, memorizing names and composers of prescribed recordings and some singing from music readers full of uninteresting songs which we tapped out while the smarter children sang the syllable names. Does it sound unappetizing? It was.

The imaginative teacher who deplored this system was given little sympathy from any music supervisor, and was urged to get to work on those required records so that her class wouldn't disgrace the school if "Dr. So-and-so" came to observe a lesson. Consequently the teacher taught what she disliked and passed her lack of enthusiasm on to the children.

The more modern approach may equip the student with fewer facts but give him a more genuine feeling for music. There is a middle ground where many songs, many records, much discussion and a learning of necessary facts all combine in an appreciation—an *understanding*—of music. Facts can be forgotten, but true understanding never leaves children, and they will have something very precious all their lives.

What musical concepts should be stressed?

1—MOOD

Even in early grades little children learn to compare and contrast musical games, songs and recordings. When the words are gay the music is fast and bright, and when there are no words a child—with some encouragement—can guess the *mood* the music is meant to convey. Sad or sleepy music is usually soft and slow. The child is learning about Mood and, although he is not yet conscious of it, finds a flute or a violin more suitable to a certain kind of music than a drum or a trumpet. Of course, he needs the teacher's guidance, but a smart teacher talks as little as possible—doesn't put words into a small mouth, or confuse young minds with too many suggestions. A wise teacher lets a child express his own simple thought on a subject. This he remembers. The too talky teacher he will tune out.

2—TEMPO

The small child learns the meaning of "tempo" and enjoys using such terms as "largo" and "presto" to describe the slow and fast types of music. We can begin to build a musical vocabulary in first and second grades, and add to it as the child grows in his understanding.

3—DYNAMICS—(loud and soft)

In third and fourth grades children add to their knowledge of mood and tempo. Now they not only increase the musical vocabulary to include the terms "piano" and "forte" but realize that songs in the major keys tend to make people feel happier than those in the minor keys. They notice that minor music is *usually* (but not always) slower. Under your guidance they learn to distinguish between major and minor chords played on a piano or Autoharp—or even on resonator bells. At this age children respond to major and minor largely through the mood created by the chords or song.

When we discuss reading music from books in Chapter 4, we will find that children learn to recognize the signal given in a song for increasing or decreasing the volume. In listening to music, they like to use their hands to show how the melody grows louder or softer.

4—RECOGNIZING "FORM" OR PATTERNS

As we said earlier in this chapter in the discussion of "Pufferbillies," the children came to realize that some lines of the song were alike, and some were different. Fourth graders learn to call the first line "A," and the line that is different "B." So our "Pufferbillies" song takes the form (or pattern) of A-B-A, for lines one and three are alike. Line two is different so we call it "B."

When Miss Miller's fourth graders studied "form" in their songs, Tina said that repeating the melody seemed to tie the song together, and Jim said he thought the change in melody made it more interesting. These two youngsters, in their own words, stated what musicians realize—repetition gives a feeling of unity and variation makes for contrast.

5—HARMONY

Children in the early grades like to sing a song while the teacher plays a harmony part a third higher or lower on the resonator bells (or piano). As they *listen* to music it becomes evident that songs have an accompaniment; that two instruments play different tunes at the same time for a pleasing effect; that they, themselves, as they sing a round, produce the same satisfying harmony.

All these discoveries pave the way for part singing in a later grade, and also for the greater appreciation of the recordings of singing and instrumental groups.

The pleasures of listening

Not all listening should be the quiet, polite audience kind. There are many times when we want our children to respond actively, physically. They respond to a rhythmic beat as in a march or dance. They "direct" the orchestra as they learn two-part (duple) and three-part (triple) beat, or as the music increases or decreases in intensity. It is important that children be encouraged to take an active part—*when listening is supposed to be active.*

Just as important to their musical education is learning to be a member of an audience—a member in good standing who does not infringe on the right of others to enjoy listening to music.

To achieve an even balance between the two types of listening we must (1) permit and encourage *active, physical* participation in listening and responding to music when that is the order of the day, and (2) teach our children an appreciation—an understanding—of music so that they may enjoy quiet periods of listening and permit others to do the same.

LISTENING TO MUSIC FROM BACH TO THE BLUES

1—Children are surrounded by music of one kind or another everywhere they go.

2—It is up to the teacher to help a child separate good music from the sensational. By training the ear we teach children to appreciate the fine points of mood, tone, melody, harmony and rhythm. This is a very gradual process.

3—Background music can be used to advantage in a variety of ways: (*a*) to encourage a quiet rest period; (*b*) as a quiet, comfortable setting for drawing or painting; (*c*) to smooth over awkward periods; (*d*) to create an interest in good music. (Making your own tape of background music is most rewarding.)

4—When children show interest in certain background music it may present an opportunity for "guided" listening.

5—Small children learn that music can be loud or soft, fast or slow, pleasant or unpleasant to the ear.

6—Older children like to experiment with harmony of voices and instruments.

7—Interest in the orchestra (or band) may begin with the simple classroom instruments children like to play.

8—Teach the understanding of *one* orchestral instrument at a time. Listen to recordings featuring this instrument; study its appearance. Then learn about other members of the same family, for example, all the strings, all the woodwinds, all the brass.

9—Use not only classical music in your guided listening, but carefully selected "pops" numbers, also. This is true of the songs your children learn as well.

10—Introduce the composer when the children's interest in him is apparent.

11—Instead of many boring *facts,* stress the *concepts* of (*a*) mood, (*b*) tempo, (*c*) dynamics, (*d*) form (or patterns), (*e*) harmony.

Part Two

NOW THAT YOU HAVE
MORE CONFIDENCE

Your children are enjoying the relaxation of rhythm songs. You and they have a variety of familiar melodies in the "Song Bag." You listen together to recordings with a pleasure and appreciation not possible before. There is a growing understanding of the place of each instrument of the orchestra and of its contribution to the beauty of a selection—just as our voices join together to contribute to the beauty of a song.

Teaching children to read music sounds like quite a task, but you have progressed to a point where you feel able to tackle a slightly more difficult problem. Acquired slowly, step by step, the ability to read music grows with the experience of doing it and the process is *not* difficult if a teacher takes time to build the necessary foundation.

Part singing and instrumental accompaniments are the fruits of our earlier efforts and can be among the most satisfying areas of a music program.

chapter 4

Teaching Children
to Read Music

No discussion of teaching music to children would be complete without paying homage to Lowell Mason (1792–1872). Mr. Mason devoted years of his life to the training of teachers in "Music Conventions" so that they, in turn, might bring good music to their classes.

After a long struggle with stubborn Yankee school boards Lowell Mason managed to introduce music study to the public schools of Boston. He worked without pay for some time—often supplying the necessary material himself. His method was similar to that of Pestalozzi, the European educator, who startled his own educational world with revolutionary ideas respecting the natural order of individual development in children. His insistence on the importance of concrete experience has been re-emphasized by more recent educators.

Mr. Mason went about his work training children to sing and presented a concert that set doubters back on their heels. With the opposition thus overcome, he was placed in full charge of music in the Boston schools and given four assistants. Soon Washington, D.C. followed his lead and then St. Louis—and music was on its way. It was a thorny path, to be sure, but it had started. Books were scarce and so were trained instructors. (Does this have a familiar ring?) However,

Lowell Mason's ever more popular music conventions were doing the job. He not only trained people to teach music to children but gave teachers the opportunity to discuss problems that arose in this new field.

Proof of the enormous popularity of his music conventions is shown by their attendance. The first one in 1834 boasted *twelve* delegates and in 1849 there were *one thousand* from all over the East. In 1876, shortly after Lowell Mason's death, the Music Teachers National Conference was formed.

Reading music is similar to reading words

There is much similarity between learning to read words and learning to read music. The speed with which children learn to do each varies greatly from one little individual to another. One child at home uses words and phrases—even sentences—earlier than his brother or sister and, for a variety of reasons, learns to read sooner.

And it's the same with music. The young child at home who enjoys singing is ready to read music sooner—wants to read music from a book and often pretends to do just that.

Time and again as we discuss music reading readiness this similarity will be apparent. There is a definite "readiness" and how much simpler it would be if all the children in one class were ready at the same time. But they're not! In the average heterogeneous class we have a difference in word reading ability of from ten months to three years—or more—and we adjust our teaching accordingly. It may seem more of a problem to adjust our teaching to the difference in readiness to read music, particularly if one feels he hasn't sufficient training—but you can do it.

When do children begin to read music?

There is no specific grade of which we can say, "Children are now ready to read music from books." If they have sung many songs, acted out songs, responded rhythmically to music; if they have learned to beat time as they sing and are familiar with the many moods of these songs, children are ready to read music.

It would be a great mistake to assume that your new class is able to read a song from a book just because it is a fourth, fifth or even sixth grade. I have met many a group, smart enough in its general studies, that knew little or nothing about the staff, the G clef or syllable names.

To have introduced such facts to them without a great deal of preliminary groundwork would have dealt a fatal blow to the goal the teacher had in mind. If you met a like situation in math, reading or composition you'd be very much concerned.

If, for one reason or another, your new class seems to have been shortchanged musically it is up to you to give them the experiences needed—experiences discussed at length in Chapters 1 and 2 on Rhythm and Singing. Children must "feel at home" with music. They must be able to relax as they sing—to act out a rhythmic selection unselfconsciously. It is important that children like and accept music before the teacher attempts the next step—reading it.

In order to familiarize yourself with the background your present class should have had in music training, we'll go back to the beginning. This, in combination with the suggestions in Chapters 1, 2 and 3, will bring you to the point where you can proceed with confidence with a third grade—or a sixth.

In almost any class there are a few who have had more music training than others. As we go ahead with our discussion we will find ways to use the talents of the more experienced—or perhaps the more gifted. We will not waste what they have to offer.

Preparation for music reading begins in first grade

Miss Baker's first graders have been enjoying "Five Little Chickadees" (see below). The numbers 5-4-3-2-1 are shown on the chalkboard and it's a great privilege for a child to be asked to point to the corresponding number as the song proceeds in its verses from 5 chickadees to 1.

Without saying anything about it, Miss Baker starts to clap—just *one* clap for each measure—as the children continue to sing:

"Three little chickadees|Looking at you|One flew away and|
    (CLAP)   (CLAP)   (CLAP)
Then there were two"
    (CLAP)

Almost automatically the children follow their teacher in this beat, for it's natural to want to express the rhythm of a song. Noticing that some of the children seemed to beat four times to the measure—

1   2   3   4
"Three little chickadees—"

Miss Baker joins them and finds that four beats to a measure is easier for everyone and seems to be more satisfying—if one can judge by the expression on the faces. So the whole song is repeated with four beats instead of one to the measure and the experiment is a success.

Since little children's attention span is very short the teacher feels

Five Little Chick-a-dees

1. Five lit - tle chick - a - dees, peep - ing at the door,
2. Four lit - tle chick - a - dees, sit - ting in a tree,

One flew a - way and then there were four.
One flew a - way and then there were three.

Refrain

Chick - a dee, Chick - a dee hap - py and gay ;

Chick - a - dee, Chick - a - dee, fly a - way.

3—Three little chickadees,
   Looking at you,
   One flew away
   And then there were two.

4—Two little chickadees,
   Sitting in the sun,
   One flew away
   And then there was one.

5—One little chickadee,
   Left all alone,
   He flew away
   And then there was none.

that the next step in her plan for them can wait until later in the day— or even tomorrow. It's a temptation to keep going now that interest is high but experience tells Miss Baker not to push her luck. This next step is too important.

A "picture" of the song

The next time these first graders sang and enjoyed the beat of "Five Little Chickadees" Miss Baker said, "Would you like to see a picture of your song?"

"A *picture* of the song!" exclaimed Robbie. "Do you mean a picture of five little chickadees?"

"No, not five chickadees," answered Miss Baker, "a picture of *your song.*"

Robbie looked puzzled but the other children said, "Yes! Show us a picture." "Draw a picture for us!"

Robbie stood near Miss Baker to "lead" the class in singing. Some sang and beat time, others simply sang and still others just watched as their teacher put the picture on the board (using the side of a small piece of chalk).

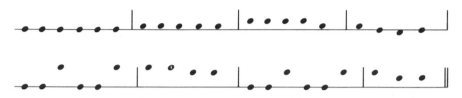

(Notice that no words are printed here. The children are just beginning to read words and there would be too much uncertainty and confusion. Attention is focused solely on the *pattern* taking shape on the board.)

There was some surprise that Miss Baker considered this a "picture," but as she pointed to the simple notes as the class sang and clapped, interest grew.

"Let me point, Miss Baker!" begged Joanne and she and her teacher led the others as they sang. Then Bill, Mickey and Maria took their turns. When Peggy started to lead the song from the picture she stopped suddenly.

"What's wrong, Peggy?" asked Miss Baker.

"What is *this* thing?" (pointing to the sign of the measure—the "bar").

"That is used to measure the song—to make it easier to sing."

Peggy went on and when she came to the next measure sign glanced quickly at her teacher and went right along to the end.

Since no one other than Peggy displayed interest in the "measure," Miss Baker decided it could wait until the subject came up again. Then the children would "discover" that measures really do measure a song—the way a man in a shoe store measures one's foot—the way a man who drives an oil truck measures the oil he puts in your tank. Measures tell you a good place to take a breath and make it easier to read a song from a "picture" or a book.

Another important discovery is made

Some child is bound to notice that the song seems to go up steps and down steps. Another may think it's like climbing a ladder. Good! Take your staff liner and tell the children to watch while you make some steps (or a ladder) for the song to climb up and come down again.

Never mind making fancy notes. As the children sing their song, put quick little marks on the proper steps (lines and spaces of the staff). It's still the *pattern* that's important—not the perfection of the picture.

If there's a question about why some notes are not on "steps" but in between, remind the class that stairs have spaces between them and so do the rungs of a ladder. The word "space" is correct and that's all they need to know right now. Keep it simple. When it's time to know more about "spaces"—when they are ready for it—you will tell them.

"Let's draw a song picture in the air"

A few of your children have had the opportunity of leading others in singing from the picture on the board. Now it's time for everybody to get in on the act, so let's draw a picture in the air.

Standing in front of the class, tell them you are going to draw another picture while they sing but this picture will be drawn in the air—so watch *very* closely. Use both hands and make your gestures large for it's important the children see that the song is climbing up and down steps. In the refrain make your "Chickadee" skips of a sixth from F to D *real jumps*. Do the same with the jumps of a fifth from F to C in the next two "Chickadee" phrases.

When the children try this with you they will probably exaggerate it more than you think necessary but let them enjoy the experience. It will impress them with the fact that the notes they see on the board really jump around and when it's time to look at music books these jumps will carry a message.

Practice beforehand

Stay after school and practice putting that "picture" on the chalk-board:

1—A few sweeps with the staff liner will make you feel more at ease but be sure the chalk is all lined up neatly before you start the operation.

2—Sing the song as you practice putting quick little notes on the staff and practice until you can do it in the tempo you want the children to use.

3—Practice in front of your wardrobe mirror as you make the "picture in the air." You *should* find out how your hands are be-having.

On the chance that one of the neighbors who hasn't gone home might find this highly amusing you can insure privacy by locking the class-room door. If you have an experienced, sympathetic neighbor it might be worthwhile asking for help.

Use the same technique with other songs

Once you have succeeded in capturing the children's interest with "Five Little Chickadees," try extending your repertoire with "Go Tell Aunt Rhodie" (a delightful song whose mock pathos even little ones can enjoy), "Pussy Cat, Pussy Cat," the refrain of "Jimmy Crack Corn," "Ten Little Indians." Not all first-year songs lend themselves readily to the introduction of music reading but you will find these five made to order.

It's never too early for ear training

First graders learn to recognize chords that sound alike, a sequence of notes in a familiar song, and repetition of phrases. Since the ability to read music depends so much on coordination of eye and ear, an early start in recognizing such similar patterns is a big step in the right direction.

The child sees you put quick little notes on the staff as he is singing a song. He comes to realize that as his voice goes up or down notes do the same thing. One child will see this quickly—for another it takes more time. Use every opportunity to reinforce the point. Once it becomes an accepted part of children's basic musical knowledge it is theirs for good.

When the children have tried a variety of songs, are confident of their ability to beat time as they sing and can use free movements to express the up and down position of the notes, show them how the song looks in your music book. It may not be as much of a surprise to them as you expect, for children have access to many books and more than likely a number of them have examined some kind of music book at some time.

Use the overhead projector

Rather than hold up your own book for inspection in front of a large group, it will be more exciting if you let the children have the fun of seeing a song they know projected on a screen.

They will want to talk about it and ask questions and everyone can see perfectly what it's all about. You may expect questions about the G clef, the sharps or flats, the time signature, the different kinds of notes. Don't ignore the questions. Neither should you go into detail at this point. Tell the children that each of these signs helps people play or sing the song just right and some day soon they, too, will learn about notes and clefs.

While the picture is projected you can sit by the machine and direct the song. (This is the great advantage of an overhead projector.) When the children have sung to their hearts' content let them take your pointer, one at a time, and (1) show the big jumps (as in the "Chickadee" song), (2) find places where the pattern of notes is repeated, and (3) point out notes that look alike.

If there has been a healthy interest in your experiment, borrow a set of music books from the second grade and, as a special treat, have the class examine them under your guidance.

Each grade builds on the experiences of previous grades

We have shown how to lay the groundwork for music reading in first grade for this is where it should begin. There are a number of reasons why this may not have been done. Very often it is nobody's fault, but it *is* up to you—in second grade or wherever you find it—to remedy the condition. If it's obvious that *any* class you fall heir to has missed out on early music training, start as far back as necessary and proceed slowly.

This is the reason we have stressed the important early training—and the need to make it up if it has not been given.

We're ready to go ahead now with the development of music reading skills through the grades, building each on the experiences that came before.

Two songs that teach many new points

There are two songs that are excellent for teaching music reading to second grade classes. The melody of the two is almost identical. Start with "Twinkle, Twinkle, Little Star" and follow that with "Baa! Baa! Black Sheep." They can be used to illustrate the following:

1—A repeated rhythmic pattern
2—Steady two-part beat
3—Progression of notes up and down the staff
4—The half note, quarter note, eighth note
5—Skips and jumps of thirds and fifths
6—Perfect pattern of the tonic chord (do—mi—sol)
7—Possibilities of accompaniment of melody bells, resonator bells, Autoharp chords or simple piano chords.

Twinkle, Twinkle, Little Star

Baa! Baa! Black Sheep

The two songs are excellent for the continuing study of the staff, the G clef and, when your class is ready, the simplest of time signatures (2/4) and the key of F (one flat). Quite a lot for two little songs to offer.

The all-important staff

The staff is all-important when learning to read music for it is the framework upon which we build so many of the new music skills that must be learned. Such skills take time and a great deal of drill is needed for there are three different categories involved:

> 1—numbers from 1 to 8
> 2—syllables from low "do" to high "do"
> 3—letters of the alphabet from A to G

Fortunately there is no rush and we can teach one new thing at a time—as we do in any other subject—relating the new point to something our children already know. Using the staff liner to introduce new facts about the staff and using the overhead projector to re-enforce such learning greatly facilitates teaching staff fundamentals.

Where shall we start?

First year children know something about the staff for they have seen it (1) on the board, (2) projected on a screen, and (3) in books.

They know that notes and voices go up and down together. They have begun to *coordinate eye and ear*.

The teacher in second grade reviews favorite songs, tests her children on their knowledge of song patterns and staff, and decides when it's wise to introduce something new.

Suppose we use the first of the two songs above—"Twinkle, Twinkle"—and see how its simplicity and steady rhythm help children learn about note values:

1—If the song is unfamiliar to the class teach it thoroughly until it can be sung with ease and assurance.

2—Put a "picture" of the song on the board as class sings it.

3—Have children use slightly exaggerated gestures in the air to show the steps—up and down—the skips between tones, two-part rhythm.

4—Project the actual song on a screen. If words are printed under the music, so much the better for these children are becoming interested in words and can see that words and music fit each other. (Your guidance may be needed here.)

5—Have class sing "Twinkle, Twinkle" from the projected song as all of you beat "1—2, 1—2," right through the song. (*Soft* clapping is good, too.)

6—Ask a question. "Peter, can you point to a note that has just *one* beat?" (Give several other children a chance.)

7—Teacher: "That little black note with only one beat is called a 'quarter note.' Susan, can you point to *another* 'quarter' note?" (Practice pointing out quarter notes.)

If someone asks about the note that *isn't* black—the half note—tell him what it is and that it gets *two* beats. If the class is still interested, go ahead and study the half note (as above). (Don't *push* any of this. Some classes can stick with a subject longer than others. Remember, small children's attention span is very short.)

8—Next time around review this slowly and patiently, for children at this age tend to forget quickly. Don't go ahead with the next step until they can recognize a quarter note—and name it—even when it appears in a different song. Here is an opportunity for the child who learns quickly to take a friend under his wing and help him find quarter notes in your songbook.

9—If you use this detailed step-by-step plan and review before attempting anything new you will find that teaching the half note and even the eighth note will present no real problem.

Teach "Baa! Baa! Black Sheep" when you're ready for eighth notes and you will find that the familiar melody and the same two-part beat help children feel at home and reassured. They'll pick up the idea easily.

2/4 time means two beats to the measure

Even if your second graders have some idea of what a *measure* is, their idea may be quite vague, so don't hesitate to re-emphasize the importance of it.

At some time when you have a song projected on a screen find out what they *do* know about measures. Right now you're studying two beat rhythm so point out—using the projected song—that each measure has *two beats:*

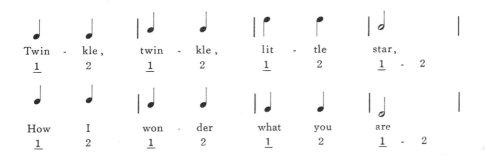

A quarter note gets *one beat;* a half note gets *two beats*. Repeat as much as necessary. *Never assume it will be remembered.*

At the same time teach the children to emphasize *beat one* of each measure. The second beat is lighter. If they learn this now it will be easy to teach the *one*—two—three beat when 3/4 time appears in a song.

There's much to learn about the staff

Up to this point first and second graders look upon the staff as some mysterious creation holding the picture of a song. They may feel there is more to this than meets the eye because older brothers and sisters—and even Teacher—sometimes use strange words without explaining them; words that don't sound like words—"do . . . mi"—what kind of language is that?

Children in second grade are old enough to learn some of the secrets of the staff, so the best place to begin is with the lines and spaces. This time, when you use the staff-liner put *nothing* on the staff—not a measure sign (bar), nor a clef, nor a time signature.

1—Ask a volunteer to come up and count the number of lines. That's easy! Anyone can count *five* lines. Nevertheless, have several volunteers count to make sure they all agree that there are *five* lines.

2—Print on the board, "The staff has *five* lines."

3—Now ask a volunteer to come up and count the *spaces.* (Looks easy, doesn't it?) It's possible that your first candidate will count correctly and find there are *four* spaces between those *five* lines. More likely he will become confused and count *below* and *above* the lines as well as between them and come up with a startling number of spaces.

At a time like this a wise teacher lets the children try to discover for themselves the answer to the puzzle. If there is too much floundering around, step in and straighten things out. In either case review frequently that a staff has five lines and four spaces.

4—Print on the board, "The staff has *four* spaces."

Leave the plain staff and the two statements on the board where you can refer to it later in the day.

There are three ways to name the lines and spaces

When the time seems right—perhaps after a game or song, but never when children are tired or restless—take your chalk and go back to the plain staff on the board:

1—Teacher: "I'm going to write a little song on this staff for us to sing. It's called a 'SCALE.' To make it easier for you and me I'm going to start it on a tiny little line below the staff. Then the song won't be too high for our voices. You'll see."

2—The teacher writes a scale *very slowly* starting with "middle C" on the "ledger" line below the staff, singing "1—2—3—4—5—6—7—8" as she writes.

3—Teacher sings with children as she points to each note (or tone) in the scale. Repeat several times.

4—Try coming down the scale (you may want to call it "coming down the ladder") counting "8—7—6—5—4—3—2—1" or singing "la-la-la. . . ."

5—Repeat until class sings with ease up and down the scale using numbers one time and "la-la-la" another. Using the complete up and down scale (see below) will make it easier for children to understand what they are singing. It helps to use hands to show the climb up the ladder and down again.

Encourage the use of a simple question and answer as you and the children climb the scale and descend. Girls can sing the question—boys, the answer. Notice that the "song" ends with the word "home." This will help when you start calling the syllable "do" the "home tone" a bit later.

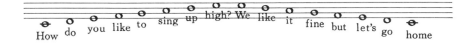

Introducing syllable names

Our second graders are becoming familiar with the staff and the scale. They count from 1 to 8 as the scale goes up and from 8 to 1 as the scale returns to the home tone.

Before introducing all the syllable names—which are really a different language—try presenting them in the following simple way:

1—Using the scale that has numerals under each tone, sing it up and down several times.

2—Tell your class to watch carefully and listen carefully as you point to something *very tricky.*

3—Point to 1—3—5 slowly and sing "1—3—5" as you point.

4—Children join you as you point to the tones. Several boys and girls take turns pointing as the others sing.

5—If you have melody bells or resonator bells use their sweet tones to accompany singing.

6—Teacher sings "do—mi—sol" and class repeats before they realize it's supposed to be hard to do. Repeat this great achievement several times.

7—Now do the same coming down with "sol—mi—do."

8—Write "do—mi—sol" and "sol—mi—do" on the staff.

9—You may want to go as far as the high "do" (do—mi—sol—do) but this can wait for another lesson if children are tired.

10—When a child asks about these new names tell him we use them because it's harder to sing using *numbers*—syllables are easier and sound better. (That's enough for him at this point.)

When you begin your next lesson review from the staff on the board what the children have learned previously:

1—Singing scale up and down using numbers
2—   "   "   "   "   "   "   la-la-la
3—   "   "   "   "   "   "   words (as in example above)
4—   "   do—mi—sol—do up and do—sol—mi—do down

If this goes smoothly try something new: put a "re" and a "fa" in their proper places and sing as you point, "do, re, mi, fa, sol" and ask the children to sing it several times. Then write the "fa" and the "re" in *their* proper places and come down to the home tone "do"—and there you are.

Jack, Betty, or Julie is sure to ask why you didn't finish the scale, so this could be the time to teach "la—ti"—and now you have it all. Sing the scale over and over using (1) syllable names, (2) words, (3) la-la-la, (4) numbers. If the class is not tired have several children take turns leading and let each one choose which way he wants the others to sing the scale.

Don't be surprised if the above plan is too much for one lesson. Watch the reaction of the children and be prepared *not* to teach all this at a sitting. There is always tomorrow. Always start with a short review of what you taught yesterday. Second graders have short memories and until these concepts become part of their thinking, daily reviews are a *must*.

Learning the *letter* names of lines and spaces

By this time your class knows that the staff has *five lines* and *four spaces*. They know that notes are *on lines* and *in spaces* and recognize the fact that notes go up and down and sometimes stay *on* the same line or *in* the same space.

Now the children are ready to learn that each line and space has a *letter name* as well as a number.

1—Put a staff on the chalkboard.
2—Put a G clef on the staff.

3—Tell the class this is called a G clef because it always curls around, comes to rest *on the second line* of the staff and *that* line is called "G." (Show them.)

4—Teacher: "Let's draw some G clefs in the air. On which line does it come to rest? Let's make another one—and another."

5—Teacher: "We use the first *seven* letters of the alphabet to name our lines and spaces. What are these seven letters?" (As the class recites "A-B-C-D-E-F-G" the teacher prints the letters on the board.)

6—Teacher: "Point to the line you know is 'G.' [Use volunteers.] How do you know that line is 'G'?"

7—Teacher: "If the second line is 'G,' what is the *first space?*" Give the necessary help and proceed as slowly as you have to with the other lines and spaces until the picture takes shape—like this—filling in as you proceed:

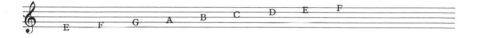

Two charts that will help you

Using the staff-liner at the chalkboard is invaluable; practice with it until you can use it easily and surely. Handy as the staff-liner is, there are frequent occasions when a previously prepared chart will save a great deal of time.

Here are two charts worth their weight in gold if a teacher takes the time to make them:

Chart A—This is actually the same staff you made on the board and used to teach (1) the staff, (2) the numbers of the tones in the scale, and (3) syllable names.

Use stiff cardboard (white, if possible) and be sure to make it large enough to be read from any part of the classroom. (I suggest 9 by 42 inches.) Since a teacher has to take storage problems into account, it would be a good idea to hinge the two halves of the chart at the center with tape. This chart needs a G clef to make your scale look more like a regular song. Put one measure sign (a bar) halfway across between the two "high do's." As you plan the chart, use light pencil first and later a black felt pen.

Chart B—Prepare a chart similar to the one you drew on the chalkboard when you taught the *letter names* of lines and
spaces. Put the G clef on the staff but there is no need to
use any bars here. Prepare the chart black on white and
as large as you feel necessary. (Nine by 36 inches is suggested.)

Charts A and B are fine aids for the drill that is so much needed as
second graders learn the new music language. Teach it thoroughly in
this grade and the children will remember it. Never rush any such new
work, and stop, review and drill whenever you see it is needed.

The Home Tone

The idea of a home tone is easy for a child to understand. A song
likes to end there—at home—just the way the child expects to go
home at the end of a school day.

But the child may have difficulty understanding why the home tone
is C in one song and perhaps G or F in another song. Tell him that
another name for "home tone" is "key-note." When our song is written
in the *key* of C our *key-note* is C, but if a song is written in the *key* of
F (as our old friend "Baa! Baa! Black Sheep") then our key-note (or
home tone) is F. Be matter-of-fact about it; tell the class only when a
change of key and key-note has to be explained. Tell them each time
it occurs and quite soon some of your pupils will be able to tell you.

Using the music reader

Introduce the music reader gradually. Children in second grade consider it a great treat when the teacher distributes books for a definite
purpose. It sharpens interest in a lesson.

Use the books sparingly at first:
1—When you have studied a song with certain interesting
musical phrases (from the board), let the class have the pleasure of identifying like phrases in a song from the music reader
—a song you will have selected in advance.

You can start very simply with a song ending in a phrase

that comes down the scale to the home tone. Tell the children where to find the song but let *them* discover the phrase.

2—When your class becomes familiar with the feel of the music reader they can use it to discover a song in the same key as they found in a blackboard song, or an identical time signature, and so forth.

There will be a class now and then that is just not ready to use a music reader. Don't feel you must force it on the children. You can do very well with blackboard, charts and the overhead projector. There are supervisors, highly trained in music, who say that music readers can be postponed to the third grade—and even the fourth—if the time is obviously not ripe for a particular group.

Reading music skills grow in third and fourth grades

Boys and girls who have had plenty of drill in such skills as we discussed in this chapter will come to the intermediate grades ready to put their skills to work. There is enough background, now that the most elementary music fundamentals are understood, to appreciate the challenge of reading music.

By no means is the child at this age ready to tackle the subject without help. He still needs drill and review of the basic concepts studied earlier. He still needs his teacher's help and the support of classmates as he sings familiar songs and reads new ones from books. He still has much to learn, but should have a good foundation on which to build what you are prepared to teach him.

It is almost inevitable that several children in the class will need special help in reading music. Have the youngsters to whom it comes easily assist you. Pair them with those who need help, as we did when we found a boy or girl in the early grades who was an off-pitch singer (Chapter 2). Frequently one child can teach something to another more easily than his teacher can. If they are together when singing or reading music (oftener, if possible), the help comes naturally and no one feels embarrassed.

Some new facts are taught in intermediate grades

Much of your music at this time is the improvement of skills taught in earlier grades—drill on the staff with its lines, spaces, number names, syllable names, the scale, recognition of like phrases. Everything the children learned has to be reviewed constantly so it becomes part of their music thinking. The music reader is now important to the lesson and the youngsters feel at ease as they use it—enjoy the satisfaction that comes with their familiarity with it.

Here are four new concepts you'll be introducing to your class:

1—Each song tells who wrote the words and who wrote the music. The name of the poet who wrote the verse is at the upper left and the name of the composer at the upper right. As your repertoire grows it is interesting to check and see if these names occur more than once. Children enjoy meeting again a poet or composer they already know.

2—A child is now able to read suggestions given by either of the above artists—suggestions for mood and tempo. He learns how to interpret the idea of such words as "Gaily," "Wistfully," "Steadily," "Brightly," "Vigorously." This is the way the person who wrote the music (or words) wants you to sing his song—and who should know better than he?

Very gradually you introduce a few Italian terms such as "legato" and its opposite, "staccato"; "allegro" which is lively—but not quite as fast as "presto." Study these as they appear in the music or as they come up in some natural way, such as a question asked by a child. Be sure the word is pronounced correctly and write it and the meaning on your music bulletin board. Have the class keep a list of Italian musical terms in their notebooks.

3—Learn the difference between a *slur* and *tied notes*. A slur is a curved line over or under two or more notes indicating that these notes are played or sung smoothly. A *tie* is more complicated for it joins two notes of the same pitch and means that the second note is not sounded. However, the time value of this second note is added to the first. Teach them as they appear in a song and review each time you find them.

4—There is a distinct relationship between poetry and music. The *rhythm* of a poem dictates the *tempo* of the music. The *mood* of a poem is carried over into the *sound* of its music.

Another fact: a musical phrase is usually one line of a poem. Probably the most practical and most enjoyable way to teach this concept is through choral speaking. Let's take a concrete example—suitable for use in third grade—and see for ourselves how smoothly the relationship between poetry and music develops.

I Can't Spell Hippopotamus

(Words and music by J. Fred Coots)[1]

I can spell "Hat," "H-A-T,"
I can spell "Cat," "C-A-T,"
I can spell "Fat," "F-A-T,"
But I can't spell Hippopotamus.

I can spell "Top," "T-O-P,"
I can spell "Hop," "H-O-P,"
I can spell "Mop," "M-O-P,"
But I can't spell Hippopotamus.

"H-I-P-P-O" I know, and then comes "P-O-T,"
But that's as far as I can go
And that's what bothers me, Gee!
I can spell "Dog," "D-O-G,"
I can spell "Log," "L-O-G,"
I can spell "Hog," "H-O-G,"
But I can't spell Hippopotamus.

This is a "fun" poem and children like it. A little nonsense now and then is good for all of us. After the class has become thoroughly familiar with the poem, talk with them about the possibility of presenting it as a choral speaking number. Under your guidance the children can plan what parts would be better spoken by one person, where a group should speak and where a chorus of all the voices would be most effective.

Here is the way one group of children presented "I Can't Spell Hippopotamus" as their contribution to a third year assembly program:

Leader—I can spell "Hat,"
Chorus—"H-A-T,"
One girl—I can spell "Cat,"
All girls—"C-A-T,"
One boy—I can spell "Fat,"
All boys—"F-A-T,"
Chorus—But I can't spell Hippopotamus.
    (same plan for "Top," et cetera)

Girls—"H-I-P-P-O" I know, (Boys) and then comes "Pot,"
Girls—But that's as far as I can go,
Boys—and that's what bothers me,
All—Gee!
    (Recite "I can spell 'Dog,' " and so forth, same as "I can spell 'Hat,' " and so forth.)

---

[1] Copyrighted by Toy Town Tunes, Inc.

Now the teacher asks, "If this poem were sung, what kind of music would you expect to hear?" Ellen says, "Happy music." Most of her classmates agree but Joey says that maybe the "But I can't spell" parts should *pretend* to be just a *little* sad and the children agree with this. They become aware of *mood* as an integral part of poetry—and of music.

We know there is a great difference in readiness to read music and third grade children are just beginning to experiment with it. With this in mind it is usually preferable to use your overhead projector so all can study the song together. When youngsters see *music* and *familiar*

I Can't Spell Hippopotamus

words at one time and can discuss it under your guidance there is an aura of confidence that helps greatly.

1—Talk about something the children know, such as measures— which truly "measure" our song and make it easier to read.

2—The time signature (¢) may be new to the class. Tell them it means four-part time cut in half (cut time) and see if some child can come up with the thought that this means *two* beats to a measure instead of *four*.

3—Children "talk" the song while teacher beats 1-2, 1-2.

4—Children talk the song as *they* beat 1-2, 1-2. Be sure they know what the rests mean in the measures and why the rests are there.

5—Unless some child is quick enough to notice the similarity of phrases (measures) 1, 3 and 5, and 2, 4 and 6, it will be up to you to bring this interesting fact to the attention of the class. Let them talk about it and try to find more *like* phrases (measures).

6—Teacher plays first part of song on an instrument (or sings it or plays a tape made specially for this lesson).

7—Children repeat. (There should be little difficulty, for the song practically sings itself.)

8—When the children begin to feel more at ease with the new song and can really enjoy it, the time has come to talk about note values and the different kinds of rests. Don't hurry this for it's more important to learn the song *first* as an interesting unit and later go into the study of details.

9—The *repeat* sign in line four may be new to your class. The only thing they have to know about it is that this is a *repeat* sign, which means that we go back and *repeat* the music we have just sung except that now we sing the *second* stanza of our poem. Most children will understand it easily—but point it out anyway the first few times around.

10—This is a perfect song for illustrating *"Form."* The opening eight measures we can call "A" and the second eight measures "B," for they are different. The final eight measures are the same as the beginning so we call them "A" also. Now we have the form (or pattern) of A-B-A.

11—If someone inquires about the flat appearing in the second and in the last lines, tell him it's called an "accidental"—for that's just what it is.

12—Encourage the children to use some rhythm instruments to add to their enjoyment of the music. One class used rhythm sticks

and a light drum beat to emphasize the spelling of each word
(H-A-T, C-A-T and so forth).

13—The class followed the same plan for individual, group and
chorus singing that they had used for the choral speaking of this
fun poem.

Strengthen children's concept of music reading in 5th and 6th grades

If your school has a well-planned music program—and such a program is effectively carried out—fifth and sixth grade music should be a
most enjoyable time for teacher and children. This is the ideal situation
and rather rare. Somewhere along the line there is almost certain to be
a weak spot and it's the teacher's job in later grades to discover and
strengthen such weak areas.

When a new class comes to us we want to find its ability in each subject area. There are record cards that tell us how individual children
have progressed in math and reading, science and social studies—and
we group our pupils accordingly to make teaching more meaningful.

Music is different. Classroom music is something that requires cooperation from all—each one contributing his share for the common
good. Some sing better—but everyone sings anyway. Some who are
more alert—learn facts more easily—enjoy helping a classmate.

One of the most refreshing aspects of classroom music is this: *each
child has something of himself to offer your music program*—a perfect
sense of rhythm, a true, sweet voice, an ability to harmonize, a quick-
ness to learn new musical facts, a folk song from his native land, an
instrument he can play. Combine these talents and you can have something pretty fine.

But there are still the weak points that need attention.

Three ways to locate weak spots

1. *Singing*[2]—There is only one way to test your new class in singing
and that is to have them sing—folk songs learned in earlier grades,
patriotic music used in assembly periods, a popular ballad heard on
radio and TV so often that it is familiar to them.

    a) Do they know the secrets of deep breathing? the correct posture
necessary?

    b) Does the class follow your lead? get off to a clean start? a defi-
nite, decisive ending?

---

[2] For a fuller discussion, see Chapter 2.

c) What about expression? Do they know your signals for soft? softer? faster? more power?

Before you try teaching anything new, see how your class sings a familiar song.

2. *Reading music*—Once you find where they stand in singing familiar songs, try reading from music books. This is where most classes are weak. They may sing from a book fairly well as long as you let them sing what they know. It's possible the children can tell you about key and time signatures—perhaps even recognize old friendly skips and jumps found in last year's music reader. That's fine! At least you're off to a good start.

When you distribute new music books begin slowly with what the children know and teach any new point that presents itself as a problem.

If you find a class more or less bewildered by music readers, go back a year or more (see earlier suggestions for second to fourth grades) and teach what you must, for you really have no other choice.

3. *Try a written test*—If you want some idea of the music reading ability of this new class give them a simple test. Make your questions clear and a little easier than one might expect for the grade. You don't want to frighten the children away from the subject by giving them anything too difficult.

a) The staff: Names of lines and spaces, syllable names, how the G clef gets its name, and so forth.

b) Note values: Draw a quarter note, an eighth note, a half note. What happens when a dotted eighth is followed by a sixteenth?

c) Time signatures: What does C mean? ¢? 4/4? 2/4? 3/4? 6/8?

d) How can we find a song's home tone? (They should begin to use the term "key-note" now.)

Tell your class that this test is for your (the teacher's) benefit because you want to find out where they need help and this is a good way.

Check the papers and use the information in your teaching. This *is* a good way to find where help is needed.

After a month or two, repeat the test and see how you have succeeded.

New facts you will probably have to teach

1—There is a trick to finding the key-note of a song. It's a rule, rather than a "trick," but so few children seem to have learned it that they tend to remember the rule if it is presented to them as something special:

> "The sharp farthest to the right in the key signature is always 'ti' (or 7). To find 'do' (the key-note) count *up* a half step."
>
> *And for flats*
>
> "The flat farthest to the right in the key signature is always 'fa' (or '4'). To find 'do' count *up* 5 tones or *down* 4 tones."

Of course, this will take time to sink in and the children will need many examples of how it works. You will find them rather intrigued with the idea and they seem to remember this more easily than much more simple facts.

Here are a few examples that show how the rules work:

2—Minor chords:

It is rather difficult for children of elementary school age to understand the technicalities of the differences between major and minor scales and chords. But they can *sense* the difference in mood. The major is brighter and establishes the kind of mood children enjoy in their songs. The minor is often sad and at first may sound strange to young ears.

When a song in a minor key is played for your class find out if anyone noticed something different about it. One may say it sounded sad; another, that it was spooky; still another child may think it was beautiful. Minor music can be all of these.

Take your resonator bells and play the C major chord (see below). Now play A-C-E and watch for its effect on the children. Encourage them to talk about the difference in the chords. Play the chord G-B-D —then, change it to B-E-G for a completely different mood.

When several members of the class have had the chance to try resonator bells on these chords show the children how to sing them. Group one sings "loo" on C and holds the note. Group two sings "loo" on E and holds it. Group three sings "loo" on G and holds it. Quite effective! Try the same using notes A-C-E. You can illustrate the difference between major and minor painlessly.

Play the record, "Go Down, Moses." The children hum along—or sing without the record if they know this beautiful spiritual. Ask— "Why is a minor key just right for this song?" "Why are many folk songs sung in minor keys?" Find other folk songs in the minor.

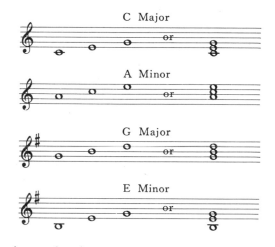

3—Teach this timesaving fact:

Using the blackboard or a chart of the scale with the numbers 1 to 8, teach your class that—

when *1* of a scale is on a line, then *2* is always in the next space . . . and. . . .

when *1* is in a space, then *3* and *5* are always in spaces. . . .

Sounds simple? It is, once the children understand it.

4—Another useful chart:

It will be helpful to you and your fourth to sixth grade classes if you have a black and white chart showing *one octave* of a piano keyboard. Ask for such a chart, but if it is not forthcoming make it yourself. The children's music readers probably have one for individual use, but it will be worth little unless they understand its meaning. On your chart show the white and black keys and name the white ones. The sharps and flats (black keys) can be named as you need them. Use this to teach whole tones and half tones.

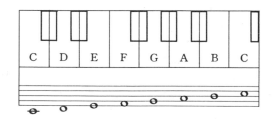

Some additional points on reading music will be discussed in later chapters. For example:

1. Part singing—discussed in detail in Chapter 5. Although much part singing is enjoyed without books, a whole new skill is required when the time comes to read parts from a staff.

2. Learning to read chords is important as children use instruments to enrich their classroom singing (Chapter 6). They will learn to recognize certain chords such as the I, IV and V7 chords which become part of their music language and are in daily use.

3. Chapter 8 discusses the ways in which music helps make a child aware of other people, other cultures, other areas of study.

   a. Learning about the pentatonic (five-toned) scale helps a child understand the distinctive quality of American Indian music which was such an important part of their religious and secular lives.

   b. The exciting rhythms and gentle folk songs of our Latin-American neighbors—music that expresses the work and play of so many people—is fast becoming incorporated with what we think of as "our" music.

   c. Children understand and enjoy syncopation as they learn more about jazz which is considered a truly American invention. The people who contributed to this "American" music have long, interesting, varied histories.

   d. Math and music become inseparable as fractions and time signatures take on a true relationship.

None of us ever learns all there is to know about reading music. The basic essentials are taught to our pupils as they are ready to accept them but the subject can continue to grow for a lifetime.

YOU *CAN* TEACH CHILDREN TO READ MUSIC

1—Children vary in their readiness to read music just as they vary in their readiness to read words.

2—There should be an ease and familiarity with songs and rhythms before a child attempts to read music.

3—First graders enjoy a "picture" of a familiar song. The teacher draws on the board (while children sing) a very simple "picture" of the notes as they ascend and descend.

4—At another time use the staff-liner to make a "ladder" for the song. Put in measure bars to make it easier to read.

5—Drawing a picture of a familiar song in the air emphasizes the steps and skips.

6—A growing coordination of eye and ear is necessary to read music successfully.

7—You will find the overhead projector a great help in preparing young children to use music readers. It is a good way to introduce the measure, time signatures and note values.

8—Teaching the staff, slowly and carefully, is an essential part of preparation for music reading. There are numerals from 1 to 8, syllables and letters of the alphabet.

9—You need charts of the staff showing lines and spaces, syllable names, letter names. If they are not available you can make them.

10—When books are introduced, use them first for recognizing like phrases, songs in the same key, identical time signatures. Give children time to "get the feel of the book."

11—Third or fourth grade is early enough to start real reading of notes and songs from books. Don't hurry it. Children need plenty of background and drill.

12—Use the assistance of children who can read music easily to help others who take longer to learn.

13—Children in fifth and sixth grade should be ready to enjoy reading music. If you find this is not the case, go back as far as necessary, teach the facts and drill on them—for you have no other choice.

chapter 5

Teaching Children How
to Enjoy Part Singing

We are born with a built-in love of harmony—whether it's for a pleasing combination of colors in a sunset, a tasteful arrangement of furnishings in a room or the sound of a good barbershop quartet. They all strike a responsive chord in us. We find them good.

If you have had the opportunity of harmonizing with a group around the piano, you know the joy that such participation brings.

Musically unskilled children like it, too. Some of them seem to be "naturals" at harmonizing—but almost any child can learn. In the field of harmony the ear is the guide and the more experience we give our guide the more efficient it becomes.

Awareness of harmony comes through listening

Although first graders vary greatly in aural ability they enjoy listening, under the teacher's guidance, to carefully selected recordings. The harmony of voices and instruments is pleasing to them even though there is little awareness of why this is so. It just *is*.

Here are several ways in which a teacher of small children can help them gain an understanding of what harmony is—become familiar with the satisfying blending of musical tones.

(*Note*): It is unnecessary to emphasize the word *harmony* at this time or even the word *chord,* but the magic of the chord is the key to harmony.

Learn to use at least one chording instrument

1—*The piano:* Don't panic and say, "I could *never* learn to play the piano!" You could, but you don't have to. Any teacher can learn to *use* the instrument well enough to give children pleasurable instruction in singing and get a great deal of satisfaction from it for one's self.

All you need learn is how to play a few chords at the right time. Let's take some examples:

If your song is in the key of C, the tonic chord is C-E-G, with possible inversions of it such as E-G-C or G-C-E.

In the key of G (one sharp) you have G-B-D and B-D-G or D-G-B.

The key of F (one flat) has the tonic chord F-A-C and A-C-F or C-F-A.

You can vary the chords used to accompany the children's singing with an occasional arpeggio that turns a simple little song into something exciting. An arpeggio is nothing more than the three or four notes of a chord played in succession (as on a harp) rather than simultaneously.

Practice beforehand and the children will love it—will look forward to their next experiment in harmony. If you learn the chords well you can watch facial expressions as the youngsters sing and you play. Try it. Children may not know much about the mechanics of harmony, but its pleasing effect on them is obvious.

2—*The Autoharp:* It may be that using a piano is impractical because of its location—not too many classrooms can boast of their own instrument. But even if you can—and do—use the piano in singing, familiarize yourself with the *Autoharp*. There are models with five push-button bars and others with twelve. (If you have anything to say about its purchase, get a twelve bar model. The possibilities are much greater.) In lower grades the smaller one will serve well, but in intermediate grades you will want to use the twelve bar model.

An Autoharp looks much like a zither and has strings that can be tuned like piano strings. It is simple to play. With one hand you press the button for whatever chord is desired and strum across the strings with a pick in the other hand. It is an effective accompaniment for singing and is becoming very popular in schools and homes.

In first grade the *teacher* uses the Autoharp. Some children can learn to play the simpler chords quite early in their school careers. All of you will enjoy its lovely chording.

3—*Resonator bells:* The tone of these "bells" (actually a set of musical bars) is sweet and true, and you and the class will get much satisfaction from their use. One model is always intact and individual bars cannot be removed for children to play at their desks. The more effective model is one that permits individual tone bars to be removed as needed. There will be times when you want to distribute one bar each to three or more children who will play the harmony as the class sings. This is rarely tried in early grades, but third and fourth—and higher—grades can handle it well.

One great advantage of resonator bells is that they do not get out of tune. Another advantage is that you can accompany the children's songs by playing a soft, pleasing harmony an interval above the melody. It's easy to do and is a delightful way to introduce youngsters to the world of harmony.

4—*Use your own singing voice:* A teacher need not be an accomplished singer to hum a soft harmony to a song children know and like. Practice your part, of course, but some time while the class is singing, without any preliminaries or explanation, just start humming along a third above the melody. It's very effective. Children love it. When you're more experienced, compose your own descant. Keep it soft. Keep it simple. There may be a child who can hum along with you. If he's gifted with a sense of harmony he (more often "she") can be a great help.

5—*Use recordings:* When you play some of those records we talked about in Chapter 3, call the children's attention to the harmony created by two violins or a flute descant or two trumpets playing an interval of a third apart. The more we are exposed to harmony the more aware of it we become. You will find that not only the class, but you too, will listen more carefully, anxious to share with others a particularly lovely passage. With experience a listener can say, "Why, that's played in thirds (or sixths)!" "That's a descant!" "Can't we try that too?"

Begin simply. As you and your class listen with a better trained ear you will gain in understanding and appreciation of harmony.

A good music background is necessary for part singing

All we have been discussing in past chapters—rhythm, singing, listening, reading music—is vital preparation for appreciating harmonic effects and for handling part singing. Ideally, the concept of harmony begins to develop in the earliest grades as little children listen to and experiment with the *magic chord*—the key to harmonic experiences.

But what if this necessary background is missing? Can a teacher go right ahead with, for example, a fourth year class and teach the descants, two-part songs and rounds he wants his class to enjoy? Music specialists advise against it, for if background is lacking your efforts are likely to fail and possibly turn your class against any such attempts you might make in the future.

Here we are faced with the same problem teachers meet when children come to them below grade in math or reading. There is only one answer, tired as we may be of facing up to it; *start as far back as you must and build from there, slowly and patiently.* When the subject is part singing, start with the concept of the chord.

Let's begin there in our discussion of teaching part singing. In this way you can discover what your higher—or lower—grade should have learned about harmony. Even if your sixth grade gets no farther than rounds and descants, how much better that will be than trying to force-feed them something they neither understand nor enjoy.

What should be taught in harmony in first grade?

1—*Singing:* The children learn their songs by rote, either from a recording or by hearing their teacher sing it to and with them.

When the song is thoroughly familiar, the teacher can try (*a*) humming or singing a tone a third above the home note as the song ends; (*b*) humming a very soft descant during the entire song or in one part of it particularly suited to harmony. If the children appear interested (which is likely) explain what you are doing. The next time you try a harmonic effect let your hands draw a "picture"—one hand draws the children's melody while the other, just a little above it, points out the harmony the teacher is humming.

2—*Using an instrument*

(*a*) Piano: Again, taking a familiar song, try some of the simple chords suggested earlier to accompany the children's singing. With a little practice you can add to your repertoire of the "one" (or "tonic") chord which is always written "I" with an occasional IV chord (the 1-4-6 notes of the scale) and, letting the ear be your guide, the interesting V7 chord which uses the "ti" tone of the scale and requires the reassuring answer of the "I" chord.

(*b*) Autoharp: In first grade the teacher accompanies the singing. Although the autoharp is not difficult to use you will find it too complicated for small hands. In addition to this, the fact that suggested chords are often written above the music tends to make it too hard for a first grader to act as accompanist. Let your class become familiar with the Autoharp—its appearance, its sound—a friendly, sweet-toned instrument that they, too, will soon be playing.

(*c*) Resonator bells: If you have the type of resonator bells that can be removed from the case, teach children how to use the 1, 3 and 5 tones, under your direction, to accompany class singing. Not all six-year-olds are ready to assume such responsibility, but let everyone have a chance to try. Those who find it difficult can always help out with rhythm sticks or a triangle. (See Chapter 6.)

Second year experiences with harmony

In second grade we continue with the concept of the chord as the root of harmony. Now you will find several in the class who can hum the "3" or the "5" tone of a closing chord along with you. There will be some who do not have such keen coordination of ear and voice control but who are perfectly able—and happy—to create a pleasing effect with the "3" or "5" tone bar of the resonator bells. Give everyone a chance to contribute to the harmony of a song. You will find that the majority of the class, at this time, will sing the melody, a few will hum the harmony with you and as many as six or eight will show some ability with resonator bells. Everyone contributes. Even the small group of children that still isn't able to sing on pitch can join in the fun with rhythm sticks, triangle or sand blocks.

Let's see how this might work out in your second year classroom. We'll take an old favorite, "Go Tell Aunt Rhody," which is fun for all ages and can be used and enjoyed in second grade or at an adult "sing-in."

Go Tell Aunt Rhody

2—The one she's been saving——To make a feather bed.
3—She died in the mill-pond——Standing on her head.
4—The goslings are crying——Because the goose is dead.
5—Repeat first verse.

(∧ ∧ ∧   use triangles here)

Have you tried an "ostinato"?

Interesting word, isn't it? In Italian, "ostinato" means *stubborn* or *obstinate*. American jazz made good use of it during the boogie-woogie period as pianists ground out a "stubborn," repetitious, seemingly never-ending bass. An ostinato occurs most frequently in the bass but is very effective in children's songs also. This can be achieved with rhythm instruments or vocally and an interesting musical experience would be a combination of melody (voices) and an ostinato of voices *plus* rhythm instruments.

Take the example of "The Diesel Train" available in Book Two of the "Growing With Music" series.[1] Here you have a simple melody rising measure by measure as the train gathers speed. Eighth notes in the accompaniment by rhythm sticks and sand blocks move along briskly to give the sound of busy wheels. While one group sings, a second group uses rhythm instruments and a third group adds to the effect of rapid movement with its own ostinato of ♪ ♪ ♪ ♪ ♪ "ch - ch - ch - ch - ch ♪ ♪ ♪ - ch - ch - ch -" eight times to the four beat measure. If this goes well,

[1] H. Wilson, W. Ehret, A. Snyder, E. Hermann, and A. Renna, *Growing With Music.*

have still another two or three children experiment with a slower

𝅗𝅥   𝅗𝅥   . Lots of fun for everybody.
"choo - choo"

Rounds and canons

As children become accustomed to the idea that songs are not always sung in the same way, that there are question and answer songs, that the teacher sometimes hums a different little tune while they sing and that instruments add pleasing effects, they are prepared to investigate still another type of musical composition.

Rounds and canons are quite similar and it's not necessary to explain the difference in their structure to your class because it is slight.

When singing a canon, each part begins in a way that overlaps the one that precedes it. For example:

Old Texas

2—They've plowed and fenced my cattle range,
And the people there are all so strange.

A *round* does just what its name implies—it goes round and round. One group starts the music; a second group begins at a given point (usually labeled "II") as the first part continues the melody. A third group joins at "III," and so on. (In third grade, limit your parts to *two*.) When the singers have gone "round and round" as often as they wish, the groups start to drop out in order until the last to begin is the last to stop singing.

Two very familiar rounds are "Row, Row, Row Your Boat" and "Frere Jacques," favorites of generations of school children. Here's a picture of the way in which your third graders would sing a round:

Before you tackle two parts in any round, make certain that *all* the children are completely familiar with both the words and music. Then:

1—Children sing while you alone take the second part softly.

2—Select a few good singers to take Part II with you.

3—Repeat this, beating time so Part I doesn't run away with the song.

4—Divide your class into two groups.

5—*Teacher* selects a good leader for each part.

6—Decide how many times the round will be sung. Once? Twice?

7—Teacher starts each group, then walks around to help.

8—Talk it over: too fast? too loud? how can we improve it?

There is a natural tendency to out-shout the other group. Talk this over with your class. Let them discover why it's a good idea to "hear" the other singers while singing one's own part. In true part singing we must learn to listen always to the other parts, and rounds and canons are a good medium for achieving this.

If you run into trouble it may be that your class is not quite ready for such a big step. Here's something you can try:

1—Divide the class into four groups with at least two of your best singers in each group.

2—Draw a picture on the board to explain how the following song will be sung.

3—Give the pitch "do" to group one. Sing and *hold* four slow beats.

4—Give the pitch "mi" to group two. Sing and hold three slow beats.

5—Continue with groups three and four.

6—Now! "Listen to the pitch"—"Take a breath!" Group one starts on "do," then continues as below.

7—Next, reverse the process (see below).

8—Encourage children to put words to tones—increase difficulty bit by bit.

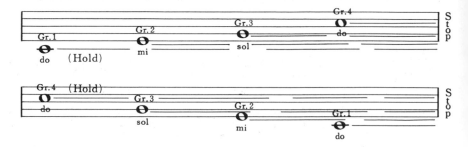

The round, "Frere Jacques," is sometimes found under the titles, "Are You Sleeping?" or "Brother John." If you want your third graders to sing the French words, it's a good idea to wait until the round is well learned in English and then experiment with another language. When children are older this is no problem. Right now the "round" feature is enough of a challenge.

Book IV of the *Growing With Music* series[2] suggests an interesting way of singing "Are You Sleeping?" Those children who do not sing the actual round introduce it with "Ding, ding, dong" for two measures using the tones "do, sol, do"—and continue this "Ding, ding, dong" until the end of the entire round. So you have your Part I, Part II and an *ostinato* by Part III. Don't rush your class. If they enjoy a few simple rounds, let them sing favorites without too much embellishment. You can tell when—or if—they're ready for more.

Introduce the "fugue" to your class

The fugue, as most of us know it, seems hardly a subject for children, yet I have found them to be genuinely interested in the similarity between their own rounds and this more advanced type of musical composition.

Bach's (Johann Sebastian) "Fugue in G Minor"[3] is called the "little" fugue although it is not "little" in musical stature. Leopold Stokowski, a great admirer and interpreter of Bach's music, calls it "one of Bach's greatest creations." This "Little Fugue in G Minor" is so simple and clear that children can follow the "subject" of the fugue and recognize

---

2 H. Wilson, W. Ehret, A. Snyder, E. Hermann, and A. Renna (Englewood Cliffs, N.J.: Prentice-Hall, Inc., 1966).
3 Record (Capitol) Bach-Stokowski SP 8489.

the theme as it appears again and again with the oboe, or English horn, or when many instruments of the orchestra join in the grand finale. The great Bach puts across his message so simply that even eight-year-olds can thrill to it.

Sometimes we underestimate the ability of our children. When their interest is awakened they often surprise us.

Singing in thirds

Some pleasant, harmonic effects are achieved by singing a third above the melody and it's fairly simple to teach to children if you take it a little at a time. Using the tonic chord of the key of C (C, E, G) and dividing the class into two groups, sing the following (notice the *fermata* signs ⌒ that mean *HOLD*):

How we love to sing in thirds! How we love to sing in thirds!

You and the children can compose your own words, varying the singing by harmonizing in a slow rhythm, repeating in an increasing tempo, with the teacher or a capable child directing. Use two hands in directing, keeping them close together, one above the other, to remind the singers of the close harmony. Try this in the keys of G, D and F.

Suggestion: Combine singing this exercise in thirds with a good breathing exercise, first with two deep breaths and then with only one.

There should be another step before trying a whole song (or refrain) for it's important that children learn to sing their own part while still hearing another group singing in harmony with them. Experiment with the whole "C" chord first with three groups singing the middle C, E and G and using a resonator bell for the high "C"; next with four groups (see below). Your singers are going to enjoy that *slur* where everybody moves a third in the chord—which carries over to the following "hold." Again you can compose your own words and vary the musical phrase by changing to another key; but beware of too high a final note lest it become screechy and spoil your effect. (Few children sing well above "F.")

How do you like our CHORD?_____

Something different to try

Sing the exercises in thirds and chords by beginning *very softly* and increasing in volume each time *under the teacher's direction*. Then reverse the procedure and end *pianissimo*. If you have trained the class to follow your hand directions they will respond. If you haven't perfected these directions, here is an ideal time to practice.

It's almost impossible to give children too much of this training. Even a fifth or sixth grade that responds well can profit by getting plenty of drill. Vary it. Keep it interesting—and no one will think of it as drill.

The harmonized refrain

Although a great many songs can be harmonized from beginning to end, we find it better to teach our fourth, fifth and sixth grade classes to sing *refrains* in parts of thirds—with an occasional fifth, sixth, octave or accidental when our ear dictates it. You will find it more interesting and definitely easier to teach if the verse is sung in unison and the refrain in parts. Some songs are perfectly suited to thirds—for example, "Polly Wolly Doodle"—and others call for a descant, as in "All Through the Night" or "America, the Beautiful." Your music series books will have many songs arranged in simple parts such as thirds or descants.

Reading part music

It doesn't pay to rush children into reading music. As we read in Chapter 4, there is so much background necessary that to hand a child a music book and expect results can be fatal to your cause.

Reading *part* music is more difficult, for here we often have not *one* but *two* staffs, and unless a class is prepared for this it's confusing. A thorough acquaintance with the song, with the melody and harmony parts of it, gets your class off to a good start and paves the way to this new challenge.

It is *possible* for a fourth year group to read part music, but it is *unusual* to find children of this age who have (*a*) the background of training needed and (*b*) the ability and concentration required to make the effort worthwhile. Nine times out of ten you'll find it more rewarding to sing many rounds and descants, to experiment with harmonizing in thirds and to plan your own ostinatos than it would be to force the issue. In this way you can send on to the fifth grade a class that loves to sing, can hear one simple melody while carrying another—in short, a group ready to tackle something new in music. And how lucky to be the teacher who receives these youngsters with a background of the simple fundamentals of harmony.

We talk a great deal about the lack of enough training in subject matter, but once in a while a teacher does receive a class that is a pure joy to work with. Now one must change his whole approach lest he fail to take full advantage of the wonderful possibilities to be found in lively, interested, alert children who come his way and spend a year of their lives with a teacher.

Mrs. Delano tells us about her experiences in music with some fifth graders—an inquisitive, easily bored group that liked nothing better than to rise to a new challenge. We can get from her some ideas for our own classes and perhaps for that "gifted" child who may turn up at any time in any type of class.

"Adventures in Part-singing" by Constance Delano

"Perhaps I should start this account of my adventures in music with Class 5–3 by filling you in on my own qualifications—or lack of them —to teach music successfully.

"Mother insisted on the usual trial period of piano lessons for me, but being a practical woman decided that, after a year of very average accomplishment, the money for my lessons could be used to better advantage in some other area. I *did* learn to read music. I *could* play the scales after a fashion and learned a few of the 'pieces' little girls perform on the piano.

"During the year previous to my adventure with this 5–3 class I had often heard about Mr. Barrone's interesting fourth graders and how they kept him on his toes most of the time. I heard them singing in the classroom and in the assemblies and admired their teacher's ability to do so much with nine-year-olds. However, my own problems seemed insurmountable at the time and the thought of dealing with such boundless energy made me fondly hope I would never have to become Mr. Barrone's successor. But that is exactly what happened. It's hard to tell who was more dismayed, I, who was expected to carry high the torch, or Mr. Barrone, who might see all his work come to naught.

"He is a true gentleman, and tactful. When I expressed doubts about my ability to cope with his former class—especially in music—he tried to quiet my fears with some very complimentary remarks about my teaching.

"If he can do it, I can try"

"The new class was delightful—eager, questioning, receptive and now and then critical. It had been so long since I dealt with this type of child that my first week was a combination of far-reaching plans and total exhaustion. But I loved it! We planned our social studies—and sang, reviewed the math picture—and sang, talked about everything on earth—and sang. I asked them to sing for me (coward that I am) and they obliged with rounds, cowboy songs, a familiar German waltz in what sounded to me like perfect harmony and a lovely descant with 'All Through the Night.'

"Jack seemed to have a perfect sense of rhythm and Marcia seemed to me blessed with what is boastfully called 'perfect pitch,' so they did most of the directing.

"With all this perfection it came as quite a shock when I learned that Peter and Walter couldn't hold a tune—Peter, in fact, was almost proud of the fact that he couldn't sing on pitch. 'But you should hear me with that Autoharp, Mrs. Delano. I bet I can play any chord you need on that thing!' he added. (And I found out that he could.) Walter is more shy and a bit retiring but his classmates are proud of his ability with a recorder and he can accompany a song with a sweet obbligato.

"Mr. Barrone had done a marvelous job and now it was up to me. I would try not to let him down.

Where does one start?

"I could have taken the easy way and let these children continue the fine pattern Mr. Barrone started so successfully. But here was a class with no desire to stand still and it deserved my best efforts.

"We reviewed some important facts about clefs, staffs, note values and time signatures. I found they had a fair knowledge of the essentials and could even find the key-note of a song if I insisted.

"Our next step was reading songs from the old fourth-grade music books. Not bad. The children could read a unison song and, with a little help, one that had a descant. Out came the new fifth-grade song-books—and we ran into trouble. Here we found ourselves face to face with two staffs and one of the staffs had *two parts* written on it. I re-assured the children by telling them that fifth grade is the time when most people really learn how to read music from a book.

Overhead projector to the rescue

"Taking the teacher's edition of the song-book which is larger and more flexible I put it in the good old overhead projector. Now all of us could see it at the same time and discover and discuss our difficulties. The verse of 'Cielito Lindo' is sung in unison— no difficulty here—but the refrain presented a problem or two.

"First we discussed the two staffs. I had decided not to make any

Cielito Lindo

Mexican song

unnecessary suggestions—just to see if the children could solve this small dilemma themselves. I would arbitrate if it came to that.

"Peggy—'The first two staffs are joined by a line—and so are the next two.'

"(Agreement—they should be sung together.)

"Brenda—'The measures seem to match—doesn't that mean they sort of keep together?'

"(General agreement.)

"Howard—'See the top staff in each set—it shows there are notes for two separate parts—I think!'

"John—'Well, does that mean the notes on the lower staff are sung by still another part?'

"Chorus—'Of course, silly!'

"Teacher—'That's not called for. John asked an intelligent question.'

"Peter (the chord expert)—'Look at the three notes in the first measure—D, B flat, F—they look like a chord that *should* sound right.'

"Ideas: 'Maybe it's the tonic chord'—'Let's find the key-note'—'What's the rule we learned for finding the key-note?'

"(After some fumbling around the children agreed)—'Take the flat farthest to the right and count *up five,* or *down four*—B flat! Let's find that chord on the resonator bells—um, sounds nice.'

"Teacher—'Let's try humming that tonic chord.' (Three parts)

"'Now try the last chord—the one at the end of the song—the "home" chord.' (B flat, F, D)

"Emily—'Why, that's the same chord with the notes in a different position!'

"After the class had sung the *melody* of the refrain in unison, I bravely took the resonator bells and accompanied the singing—not too terribly, either. Then four children asked if they could try humming it along with me—and we were singing *two* parts.

"Nobody wanted to stop, so we tried the melody and the lower staff descant while I played the 'thirds' on the resonator bells and Peter struck an occasional chord on the Autoharp. We were all delighted with our success.

"At our next session we worked on all three parts—first separately, then two parts and finally three. When the class agreed they felt sure of the song, Walter announced that if someone would work with him he would write a part for the recorder. Peter is figuring out his Autoharp chords and will soon be ready to enrich our production.

"This class has been an eye-opener to me. I've had a bright group once in a while but never one so eager, so searching, so alert. I've been learning right along with them. Now, when we find a song that looks a bit difficult, instead of hurrying on to the next page, we stop, study it and find out if it is really as tricky as it looks."

Mr. Meyer's sixth grade approach

This is an average class and a teacher has to work hard to get results. You have a few who are good in math, a few who are in the first reading group—you know how it is. Music is no different—results are often spotty and discouraging. The average child—most children—need constant pushing to achieve an average goal.

Once in a while something comes along that breaks the logjam—everyone's interested—and you take advantage of your opportunity. Who can foretell what may happen?

The fifth and sixth grades were planning a Spring Festival of dance and song. Parents would be invited and possibly the third and fourth year classes. A committee composed of the teachers and class officers of the fifth and sixth grades held a meeting. The suggestions offered by this committee were now being discussed in the classrooms.

Some of the dances learned during the year headed the list of suggestions, but Mr. Meyer's class displayed little interest. The half-dozen or so in 6–2 who wanted to be in the dancing seemed disappointed but were assured they could join a neighboring class that was planning to entertain with a dance. Well, what about choral speaking? Perhaps one of their poems could be polished up, dramatized and presented to the audience. This idea didn't go over either, so Mr. Meyer, wise in the ways of pre-teeners, changed the subject. He could wait.

As the next morning's opening exercises drew to a close the teacher walked over to his record player and, without a word, started playing the recording of the Mormon Tabernacle Choir singing the "Battle Hymn of the Republic." Then he seated himself at the desk and pretended to be very busy. This was not the time to show his own great appreciation of the wonderful music, hard as it was to pretend.

The music stopped. No one moved or spoke. Had he been wrong? He made himself keep on with what appeared to be an important job —didn't look up. Somebody came and stood rather respectfully beside the desk—cleared his throat nervously.

"Mr. Meyer . . ."

"Yes, Frank?" (Class president—big, overgrown, popular, team captain.)

"That song—the one you played for us—do you think us kids could sound like that? Man!"

"I'm not sure, Frank. It would be a perfect closing number for the Festival, but it would mean a lot of hard work."

"But you could teach us, Mr. Meyer. Your voice is good. You could maybe sing with us. And there's that record. We could listen to it and all. . . ."

"Let's talk with the class—see what they think," said his teacher. (Had he seemed too reluctant? Had he discouraged them?)

After consulting the class, Mr. Meyer's doubts were stilled. They would practice—they would work like anything—only, please, let's do it!

The Battle Hymn Of The Republic

There are usually some very high spots during any rehearsal time —but how very low those low spots can get. As it worked out, the Mormon Tabernacle Choir would never recognize this treatment of the "Battle Hymn." Changes had to be worked out, simpler harmonies devised, homemade rather than professional effects achieved. But this was Class 6–2's contribution to the Spring Festival, it was their own "baby" and they cherished it, taped it, took color snaps during the rendition and presented the gift to Mr. Meyer, who, said Frank, was "responsible for the whole business."

Class 6–2 doesn't mind if you want to try out their arrangement and they present it on the facing page for your use—plus a few suggestions offered with the best intentions.

Class 6–2 suggests:

1—We found the first and third verses our favorites and sang only those.

2—We used three staffs—our first experience with three.

3—The boys who sang the ostinato used the word "Drum-m-m-m" (4 beats). It sounded like a drum accompaniment. Next time we plan to use a real drum. "Ostinato" is an Italian word that means "obstinate."

4—We repeated the last chorus very softly, gradually increasing the volume, singing the "coda" *fortissimo* (ff)—two more Italian words we learned.

5—Our leader invited the audience to repeat the last chorus with us. They seemed to like it! And we hope you do, too.

How your tape recorder can help you teach part-singing

Do you ever wish you could sing two harmony parts at once while teaching music? Not a practical wish but it would help keep your children on pitch and singing their own part instead of following the lead of the nearest neighbor.

A tape recorder can do just that for you—by being a second voice, tireless, patient, and it doesn't get short of breath or drop a half tone in pitch.

Let's figure out how we can work this magic trick. Suppose we use an old American favorite, "Green Grow the Lilacs" as an example. You can prepare it all by yourself or you can use the assistance of a small group of good singers. First, and most important, your entire class must learn the melody and the words. Then prepare your tape recording like this:

1—If you play the piano—or have a friend who will help you—tape the second part which is written in harmony of thirds and fifths and which follows the familiar melody faithfully, making it much easier to learn.

2—If you don't play the piano—or don't have a generous friend available—practice the part on resonator bells (or melody bells, if that is what you're used to). Then record it on tape. You must be sure the rhythm is smooth, even and identical with the rhythm the class follows when they sing the melody.

3—Using the above tape recording, and after school hours if possible, train a half-dozen of your clear-voiced good singers to hum or sing this second part.

4—When they are sure of it, record their voices on the tape.

5—Now you can use your tape to (a) accompany the song, (b) teach Part 2 to the whole class. Have the group that recorded the tape scattered about the room helping other youngsters learn it.

6—"Green Grow the Lilacs" has a lovely descant; use the above procedure to teach it.

You will find that children respond to a more novel way of learning a second part *and* you have this tape for reference and for correct pitch whenever needed.

Why not record the finished production—melody, harmony and descant—with introduction, date and comments? Parents would enjoy hearing the tape at some future meeting. Why hide your light?

Singing spirituals

What a delightful way for fifth and sixth graders to study simple but beautiful harmonies. This is the "call and response" or *antiphonal* type of song in which the leader introduces the message and the chorus answers—usually in harmony.

Fanny Kemble, the gifted young English actress of the nineteenth century who deserted the stage to marry an American plantation owner, Pierce Butler, describes the singing of the slaves as they rowed the boats from the sea island to the Georgia mainland. According to her journal published some years later in England, these slaves seemed to be able to adjust their song to the difficulty of the job they were called upon to do. Rough seas, heavy cargoes—still they sang, not joyfully, but as though they *must* sing or the burden could not be borne. The "leader" set the pace in whatever tempo was needed and his oarsmen responded.

We have the religious type of spiritual and the true work song. Each served its purpose to make life less unbearable. Your children will be very much interested in pursuing this topic in social studies.

One of the well-known spirituals, "Swing Low, Sweet Chariot," is often arranged with the chorus at the beginning and end, with the "call and response" appearing twice in the middle of it. After the class is familiar with the whole song—without parts—try this:

1—Three boys sing, "I looked over Jordan and what did I see?"
2—Chorus, in unison, "Comin' for to carry me home,"
3—Three boys, "A band of angels comin' after me—"
4—Chorus:

Com-in' for to car-ry me home

5—When you repeat the chorus for the last time you can add a beautiful touch by doing this—

Chorus: "Swing low, sweet chariot

Com-in' for to car-ry me home____

Swing low, sweet chariot"—and end with parts as in #4.

When you and the class try the rollicking "One More River to Cross" with its fourteen verses about Noah and the animals in the ark, experiment with your own simple harmonic effects as the chorus repeats again and again "One more river to cross."

"Joshua Fit th' Battle of Jericho" is fun for all. The melody can introduce that jazzy beat familiar to most of us—you can accentuate its charm by clapping on the "off" beat—and when you reach "And th' walls come tumblin' down," make the most of its harmonic possibilities.

Chanteys

A child can really lose himself as he sings a chantey. Imagination takes over and he sees himself as a rough-bearded sailor on a white-winged schooner risking his neck as he furls sails in a high wind. Self-consciousness forgotten he heaves on the anchor or helps turn the winch. You might think that girls would find this boring, but the romance of sailing ships affects them too and they join in with spirit.

There are two well-known chanteys—completely different in style—that children seem to like especially. "Blow the Man Down" has a gusty, rolling rhythm that invites everyone to take part in its good humor. You might try an ostinato with a group of boys singing "Blow —Blow—" on the first beat of every *other* measure, another group singing the "call" and a third group the "response" in harmony. As for "Shenandoah," it is quiet and lovely and I have seen some pretty fresh kids with a hint of tears in their eyes as they sang sadly, "Away I'm bound to go, 'Cross the wide Missouri."

Barbershop harmony

There are 30,000 members of a singing society calling itself the (believe it or not) SPEBSQSA, which means "Society for the Preservation and Encouragement of Barbershop Quartet Singing in America."

Although such elaborate harmonic effects are much too difficult for youngsters to attempt, anyone who has worked hard learning his part in a song and who has blended his voice with others will appreciate and enjoy hearing the experts.

There are records available featuring quartets which are the winners of annual competitions. Give your children a treat; let them hear a recording of one of these groups—not with any idea of emulating such perfection, but just enjoying it to the full.

Suggestion: Decca—DL 8788; also "Lida Rose" from Meredith Willson's "The Music Man."

Some more favorite part songs—for children

Here are a few more songs your children will enjoy. Two are "apple-pie American," one an old French melody and the fourth a typical German waltz. How far a class goes with any one of these depends on their age, experience with music and their ability. If one youngster plays a recorder, he can add much to the beauty of "Aura Lee." Make up your own dance steps to go with "Du, Du, Liegst Mir Im Herzen" or try an original ostinato to make the realistic sound of a cow pony's hoofs while your two-part chorus sings the refrain of "Home on the Range." Some fifth and sixth year classes may enjoy learning the French or German words of the two foreign language songs, but it's better not to push this for the music is, after all, much more important.

Aura Lee (1861)

W. W. Fosdick

G. R. Poulton

Hum descant

As the black-bird in the spring__ Neath the wil-low tree,__

Sat and piped, I heard him sing,__ Sing of Au-ra Lee.

Au-ra Lee! Au-ra Lee! Maid of gol-den hair.

Sun shine came a-long with thee, And swal-lows in the air.

Home On The Range

Cowboy song

Refrain

Home, home on the range__ Where the

deer and the an-te-lope play.__ Where

sel-dom is heard a dis-cour-a-ging word, And the

skies are not clou-dy all day.__

Au Clair De La Lune

Smoothly   Early French song

At thy door I'm knock-ing, By the pale moon-light,

Lend a pen I pray thee I've a word to write;

Gut-tered is my can-dle, Burns my fire no more;

For the love of Hea-ven, O-pen now the door.

Au clair de le lune, Mon ami Pierrot,
Prete moi ta plume pour ecrire un mot;
Ma chandelle est morte, Je n'ai plus de feu,
Ouvre ma ta porte, pour l'amour de Dieu.

Du, Du, Liegst Mir Im Herzen

Waltz time   German song

You, You, in my heart li - ving, You,

You, in my thoughts too, You, You,

joy and pain gi - ving, Don't you know how I love

you!_____ Ja, ja, ja,

ja, Don't you know how I love you!_____

Du, du, liegst mir im Herzen,
Du, du, liegst mir im Sinn,
Du, du, machst mir viel Schmerzen,
Weisst nicht wie gut ich dir bin!
Ja, ja, ja, ja,
Weisst nicht wie gut ich dir bin!

What part-singing gives children

Today's child is born into a world full of the sound of sophisticated music. He hears the best—and the "worst," now and then—at the mere turn of a dial. Even the music that some of us find offensive is the best of its particular brand or it would not be available on radio, TV or recordings. There is music to please any taste no matter how unorthodox.

If we offer our children nothing but simple, uncomplicated melodies such as their grandparents learned as children, they will soon tire of the whole school music picture. The old melodies are priceless and should be taught, but we must offer more challenge than these present.

Part-singing offers such a challenge and gives great satisfaction, too. Having the know-how to read a part, being able to hold that part and join others in close harmony, planning with others new ways to make an old song more interesting, participating with the group around the piano or the guitar, gives a stimulation and warmth that modern man —and child—needs and cherishes.

PART-SINGING OFFERS A CHALLENGE

1—Man is born with a love of harmony and responds to it warmly.

2—The ear is the guide to harmony in music, and as the ear becomes better trained our enjoyment of harmony increases.

3—The magic chord is the key to harmonic effects and a teacher of young children begins there.

4—It is important that a teacher learn to use at least one chording instrument. If it is the piano, a few chords at the right time add greatly to the enjoyment of a song.

5—When using an Autoharp read the chords above a song, such as "I," the tonic chord, "IV" and "V7," and press the button for whatever chord you want.

6—Resonator bells do not have to be tuned and are effective accompaniment for a song—or can be used to teach a melody.

7—If the teacher hums a soft harmony while children sing a familiar song, it is a fine way to introduce harmonic effects.

8—Listening to recordings of voices or instruments in harmony is pleasing to children's ears and helps them discover harmony.

9—If your 4–6 grade class does not have the background of experience necessary to singing in parts, go back and teach what they must know. Begin with the concept of the chord.

10—If children learn to hum a closing chord in parts $\begin{smallmatrix}8\\8\\8\end{smallmatrix}$, play chords on the Autoharp or resonator bells, hum a harmonic part to accompany singing, they are well on their way to reading parts.

11—Rounds and canons help children learn how to sing one part and still listen to another.

12—Simple, melodious exercises built on the chord provide worthwhile drill in part-singing. Use chords or thirds and encourage a class to compose words to be sung with the exercise.

13—Instead of trying to harmonize an entire song, try singing the verse in unison and just the refrain in harmony.

14—Reading part music can present difficulties, for now we have not only two parts on a staff but often have more than one staff.

15—Using the overhead projector helps you discuss the problems of reading a part song while the entire class watches at one time.

16—A tape recorder is another help in the teaching of part-singing. When the children are familiar with a melody, record on tape, either vocally or instrumentally, a harmony part (thirds, descant, and so forth). Let this tape guide your class in learning to sing in two parts.

17—Spirituals and chanteys are an enjoyable way to teach part-singing. Both types of song use the "call and response" (antiphonal) approach.

18—Records of barbershop quartets will inspire your children to greater heights. Youngsters are not supposed to attempt such intricate harmonies, but because of their own experience they will be able to fully appreciate the beauty of music presented by experts.

chapter 6

Using Instruments
in the Music Lesson

For many, many years "music" in school meant "singing" in school. At first the introduction of any kind of music seemed to the hard-core educator a frivolous waste of time with the danger that such nonsense might take a child's mind off the importance of serious education.

Gradually and patiently Music found its way into the curriculum— and stayed there. At first it was *singing,* for this was inexpensive and children with good voices enjoyed it. The "monotones," as the poor singers were called, listened while others sang. There was little in it for them.

Why did it take so long for educators to wake up to the great possibilities of other kinds of music? In time the school orchestra began to appear as a few children who took lessons at home brought in violins, drums and trumpets. As for the piano students, *one* child *might* win the privilege of accompanying the orchestra.

A great step forward was the introduction of a free instrumental program in which children who thought they might like to play a certain instrument—or were brainwashed into it by a parent—were given group lessons before or after school hours.

Music Appreciation first appeared on the scene in a stereotyped, too often rigid program that took the life and enjoyment from it. Children have told me that this kind of music "appreciation" actually kept them from enjoying records at home and from listening to radio music because they felt all tied up with the need to memorize names, movements and composers. This may be a childish exaggeration but it does point to the many mistakes made in that kind of music training. Parents and teachers know that today's children suffer no such inhibitions. They seem able to enjoy some pretty awful stuff.

All this time the kindergarten teacher went her own way, wisely encouraging little ones to clap, sing, pound a drum, strike sticks together, ring sleigh bells—enjoy themselves. Why did music so often become a chore in the grades that followed—something to be borne with a sigh or, still worse, something to be ignored if possible?

It was high time that *all* children learned the joys of music—not only the good singers, not only the child with a fine sense of rhythm, not only the child whose parents could afford private lessons. Take, for example, seven-year-old Frankie whose small hands were ready to sandpaper blocks of wood smooth and fine. And there's his classmate, Ellen, striking any available piece of metal with a pencil or ruler, listening critically to the resulting sounds. Why shouldn't Frankie and Ellen have the opportunity to enjoy *their* kind of music—to enrich the class program with their own ideas?

Then came the great awakening. *Each child has something to offer.* He not only listens: he acts, he creates, he learns by doing. He can now acquire a true appreciation of the world of music.

In each of our previous chapters we have seen how instruments enrich classroom music through the elementary grades. Now, we will investigate some of the endless possibilities for enlarging the role of the instrument in our daily lessons. Such instruments may be fine, factory-made models—others simple, child-crafted innovations made from scrap material but dear to the hearts of their creators.

Where do you start a first grade music program?

If you are in doubt about the musical capabilities of your new first grade class, talk it over with the kindergarten teacher from whom you received the children. She knows her little charges very well and can give you some pointers. Who has a fine sense of rhythm? Who can beat the drum for marching? Who is a good leader? Have they used many instruments?

You may know from experience how easy it is for a first grade teacher to let the music program slide. There are so many other things to be taught and repeated and re-taught day after patient day, that time goes by—and whatever happened to the happy sound of music you used to hear when these same children were across the hall in the kindergarten room? Don't let it happen to your youngsters. Use music—all kinds—as an integral part of their day. Pounding a drum, or a relaxing song or game is a good way to refresh tired spirits. Little children are born music lovers, but this natural interest will fade without nourishment.

What instruments can be used in first grade?

As we found in our chapter on "Rhythms," young children enjoy using large, free movements, since their muscles have not learned the control that comes somewhat later. Small, rather intricate instruments would be completely out of place at age six, so we choose—and they enjoy—the types of instruments that require little more than a good swing of the arm and some sense of rhythm.

Start with a parade around the room using a simple recording or the classroom piano. This is familiar to the children—was an almost daily occurrence in kindergarten. Six-year-olds don't object to frequent repetition. They'll repeat something with glee until you're out of your mind. Try this:

1—"Let's CLAP—CLAP—CLAP as our feet STEP—STEP—STEP."

2—"What would make our parade more interesting—more exciting?" ("A drum!"—"Cymbals!"—"Something that sounds like feet marching!")

3—Teacher leads the parade with a drum while children follow clapping hands

4—Johnny takes the drum while teacher takes the cymbals.

Proceed slowly, letting each experience be fully enjoyed and allowing each child who displays interest in the drum and cymbals to have his turn. This may go on for days. Don't hurry it. You can gradually perfect the beat as young players become more familiar with the instruments.

Very gradually try adding a triangle—two—three, some sleigh bells, to the class band. Rhythm sticks are fun and several children will learn to use them without too much difficulty. A tambourine is an exciting addition, but teach the proper way to hold and beat it before letting it join the parade. (The tambourine head is struck against the heel of the hand—you can shake it or tap it with fingers.) If the band gets out of hand with players simply banging things without making any attempt at unity or good rhythm, STOP! This *can* happen, especially if the teacher is inexperienced. But it *has* happened to people who have been at the job for years. Don't give up and say, "No more of this!" Even with little ones you can talk things over if you remain calm.

"What's wrong with our band?"

Miss Pierson had been so confident. She had watched first grade teachers give demonstration lessons while she was a student teacher and had felt that she could do as well. In fact, there would be some changes made when Miss Pierson was in charge of a class. There was too much tiresome repetition of instructions. Surely children must get tired of hearing the same directions repeated over and over. And firmness! Was it really necessary to be so firm, so insistent on details?

Now, suddenly, here was Miss Diane Pierson faced with a seething mass of twenty-seven first graders gone completely silly, running around beating drums, cymbals—anything they came in contact with. And almost screaming. It had to be a dream. She would wake up any minute.

Miss Diane Pierson, honor student, modern and ambitious, lost her cool. When her loud, "Children! Children!" went unheard she picked up her yard-duty whistle and blew it hard. Gradually the word got around that Teacher was angry and the tumult died down. With both unbelief and the desire to cry, our model teacher sat down at her desk and her chastened charges went to theirs.

Complete silence. Quick glances were exchanged from child to child, with an occasional shy glance in Miss Pierson's direction. Finally Teacher found her voice.

"Does anyone know what's wrong with our band?" she asked in a very soft, strained manner.

Little children are pretty knowing. Not a volunteer offered a comment.

"Miss Pierson isn't angry with you. Why don't we talk over our problem and see if we can do something about it?" There was a hint of a smile but still no response. No one was going to be the first to test his teacher's sincerity.

"I'll tell you what *I* think we did wrong," said Miss Pierson, "and then you can tell me what *you* think about it. *I* think we tried to play too many instruments and we didn't know enough about them."

Heads nodded agreement.

"Perhaps," continued their teacher, "we need to learn more about marching with drums and cymbals before we start playing other instruments."

Heads continued to nod agreement. These children were taking no chances. Whatever Teacher said they would go along with.

Miss Pierson walked over to the record player.

"Let's listen to our march again," she said, "and then you and I can make some new plans."

While the record played, the atmosphere cleared a bit, and teacher and children were ready to discuss their mistakes and plan for a better band.

This young teacher learned an important fact the hard way—too much too soon is a disaster. She's smart enough to remember the rude awakening, to understand how it happened and to apply what she learned to other areas of teaching.

The importance of planning

We cannot neglect planning, whether we're teaching the use of a simple instrument, giving a lesson in math or just out for a walk in the school garden. Try to picture each step in your music plans and be prepared to change a plan if things are not working out. Let's say a first grade teacher has trained her class to sing "Jimmy, Crack Corn" as they walk in a circle. Little Betty proudly plays the triangle on the first beat of each measure. Teacher decides this would be a good time to add rhythm sticks to the song-game so she distributes four pairs to children around the circle. Ted plays energetically and keeps the rhythm of "Jimmy, Crack Corn." But Lou, Mary and Linda bang away gaily, all unaware of the importance of keeping time so their classmates can continue to sing.

Should the teacher: (a) Take away the three pairs of offending rhythm sticks and give them to other children? (b) Put the rhythm sticks away in the storage closet? (c) Stop the game and teach proper use of rhythm sticks? Some foresight, some plan of operation, would have avoided this complication.

Teach children how to use instruments

Teachers should never take for granted that children of any age are familiar with *anything*—from music to fractions to softball. Trying to present a game or a lesson without some background is a waste of time.

If you want to use rhythm sticks, show them to the children, talk about them, play them as you sing a little song, and let the children examine the sticks and try a few taps. Now the introduction has been made. Some boys and girls will be able to use the simple instrument immediately—they may have a "feel" for such things or an older child may have shown the youngster how to do it. Others will have trouble.

Add one new object at a time to the class band and try to work it out so that everyone gets a chance to experiment. Use a child who has the knack of hitting a triangle to help you train those who find it difficult. It's amazing how quickly one child can teach another. Add the cymbals, tambourine, sleigh bells. Don't hurry! Remember, children love to repeat and repeat.

As the youngsters become familiar with instruments, plan with them how each may be used most effectively. Why does a drum seem perfect for one song or game and yet sound all wrong when we sing a lullaby? Should cymbals be banged right through an entire march? What's the best way to use sandblocks if we want to imitate the "choochoo" sound of a train?

Using the Autoharp

This delightful instrument is a perfect accompaniment for children's songs. Its chords are pleasing, satisfying. In first grade the teacher plays the Autoharp herself, for small hands are not ready to manipulate it. To familiarize the class with the "feel" of the Autoharp, invite a girl or a boy, as a special treat, to strum the strings as you press the button for a certain chord. Watch his face as he strums the strings. Pure joy!

Resonator bells

Bells are useful in giving young children an idea of a high pitch, a low pitch, the black and white notes of a piano. A few of your pupils will learn to play very simple songs beginning with such tunes as "Mary Had a Little Lamb" (only three tones) and "Hot Cross Buns" (three tones).

The switch from resonator bells to piano keyboard is a natural step since the position of the keys on the piano is just the same as that of bars of resonator bells. Don't coax or press an unwilling child—you'll have plenty of volunteers to carry on. Shy, unconfident ones will want to try it sometime—perhaps in second grade. Give a reluctant child *one* resonator bar and his own hammer and point to him when that tone is to be sounded—for example, on the word "mice" in "Three Blind Mice." He may become excited enough about the whole idea to forget his hesitation.

Should small children make instruments?

Some teachers have experimented with the making of simple instruments in first grade and, like any other experiment, results vary so much that the individual must decide for himself. You are likely to find that *you*, a parent or an older brother is doing most of the work while the child's attention wanders off to another subject. There is so much discovery and pleasure in just getting acquainted with a tambourine, feeling it, shaking it, banging it—why force things?

There is the occasional child who must take apart anything new to see what makes it tick. He might be better employed sandpapering blocks than poking holes in the class drum. Your judgment, again; your decision to make.

Keeping together

A youngster with a fine sense of rhythm *shudders* when his classmate gaily comes in on the wrong beat or continues to bang away when the group has stopped playing. All children have a sense of rhythm, but it's much more acute in some than in others and it, too, has to be taught. How do we do this?

If a number of pupils are having some difficulty keeping together when instruments are used, practice with hands—like this:

a) Teacher claps as children sing "Ten Little Indians"—

> One little, two little, three little Indians
>   (clap)   (clap)   (clap) (clap)
> Four little, five little, six little Indians
>   (clap)   (clap)   (clap) (clap)
> Seven little, eight little, nine little Indians,
>   (clap)   (clap)   (clap)   (clap)
> Ten little In——dian boys
>   (clap-clap-clap-clap-clap - - -)
>   1   2   3   4   1 2-3-4

b) Teacher leads with drum as children clap and sing.

> Repeat steps as much as necessary. Appoint a capable leader for the song so you are free to walk around and help those having trouble with the beat.

c) When the class can sing and clap and follow the leader who uses the drum, introduce *one* pair of rhythm sticks. Teacher first uses sticks to add to the interest in this song-game.

d) Give sticks to a child who keeps perfect rhythm.

e) Proceed in this manner, introducing two or three pairs of rhythm sticks, *one* tambourine (to be struck on the *first* word of each line, *one* pair of cymbals to be struck on the *first* word of each line).

The above procedure may take several music lessons to perfect. Why hurry it? If any step is imperfect, repeat—practice until satisfied. When the children are weary, stop and rest or stop practice for the day. *This is meant to be pleasure, so keep it enjoyable.*

The pros and cons of rhythm bands

If your rhythm band is good, there is always the temptation to show it off. *You* may not be tempted to, but a supervisor or an officer in the PTA may be. There are few sadder sights than a group of first or second graders who are due to play that same evening for a parents' meeting. (The notice reads 7:45 but it's always 9:15.) They have rehearsed for days, making mistakes never made in ordinary rehearsals. Teacher is a wreck, with someone whose very life must depend on a successful outcome breathing down her neck. Children cry over mistakes; all the life and fun has long vanished. Work has been neglected. When the event is past, these instruments will be locked away with a sigh of relief. For what?

Rhythm bands are supposed to be fun. They are the successful result of a well-developed sense of rhythm exercised on instruments that highlight rhythm. Interclass entertainments are fine. Invite a guest or two. Add a new instrument to the band for these interclass affairs. See the interest in it and the true desire to experiment. This is what teaching is all about. The showing off is unfair exploitation.

Second graders become more skilled in the use of instruments

If a planned music program has been followed in Grade One, the teacher in the second grade finds her seven-year-olds much more capable of contributing to classroom music. Muscles haven't changed greatly—they still require the large, easy movement—so you cling to instruments that use the swing of the arm and hand. But now the players are better acquainted with drum, cymbals, rhythm sticks, and they see there's a reason for keeping together. The rhythm band is still a great deal of fun (it seems all ages get a kick out of this), but now the youngsters like to use their skills to accompany songs and poems.

Try this: Tommy is able to accompany the class as they sing "Hot Cross Buns" (to take an easy example). He uses melody bells and plays the required three notes without difficulty. Jeanne tells you her mother has taught her how to play this on the piano.

1—Class sings while Tommy plays melody bells and Jeanne plays the piano. Big success.

2—Repeat above with teacher playing "C" chord on Autoharp. Much enthusiasm.

3—Brian plays "C" chord on Autoharp with teacher's help as the above is repeated.

4—Repeat as above except that *Brian* plays the "C" chord on Autoharp while *teacher* plays it on *piano* (an octave above or below where Jeanne plays her little melody).

5—Each performer, teacher included, promises to teach one more person to take his place. (This is a very successful way to pass on knowledge. Witness the great spread of reading ability when a similar method is used in underdeveloped countries.)

If you have no classroom piano, substitute resonator bells. There's an added advantage, for these bells can be removed from their case and distributed among the children. Now you can have still more harmony, with melody bells playing a third above the resonator bells that accompany the class singing:

> Hot cross buns, hot cross buns,
> One a penny, two a penny,
> Hot cross buns.

(Melody bells)	543	543	3333–4444 543
(Resonator bells)	321	321	1111–2222 321

The teacher suggests (or children may ask for) the addition of a triangle or two, a drum (two, if you have them—one low pitch and one high pitch) and possibly rhythm sticks. Rarely will all of these be used for any *one* song, but encourage children to offer suggestions and let the class judge whether the effect is pleasing or what may need to be changed.

Learning to accent rhythm

Even at the age of seven a child can be taught to make his music more interesting by accenting a certain beat. In waltz time the accent is on beat one. Here he can use a triangle or drum for the desired effect. Perhaps a particular song is unsuited to either of these rhythm instruments, but by trial and error, teacher and class discover that rhythm sticks are perfect for the first beat in each measure.

Take a song in 2/4 time, like "Little White Duck." Let the children experiment with various instruments until they decide which one is best for accenting the "one" of the "one-two" beat. One group of youngsters trying to get just the effect they wanted for the above little masterpiece tried (a) a high-pitched drum which they discarded immediately, (b) rhythm sticks which did not give the *smooth* impression they wanted and then (c) the triangle. Some thought the triangle was good because it sounded as though their little duck were pecking away as he sat in the water. Then the group happened upon the pleasing combination of the triangle to accent each first beat and a steady accompaniment of sandblocks to simulate the gently flowing water.

Such an experience makes more of an impression on a child than being handed the sandblocks and told when to use them. Seven-year-olds become surprisingly discerning if given opportunities—discerning enough, in many instances, to recognize a poor choice and correct it. We can't begin too early to encourage intelligent criticism of music if we want our children to accept the worthwhile and reject the worthless.

We've been talking about working with classes that have received good music training. If you are not so fortunate with a new group, start where you must, even if it means using only *one* instrument, but start without delay. See that these children, in the year they spend with you, receive as much of their rightful heritage of music as it is in your power to give them. Nothing sensational is necessary. The joy comes with the discovery and understanding of these simplest of all instruments, the rhythm group.

Third grade builds on earlier experiences

Now you and your class can move ahead more rapidly with new music adventures. You have a background, a foundation on which to build. The children are more sure of themselves, have better muscular control. Often we find them more adventurous—eager to try new ideas. They now work better in groups and are increasingly more able to enjoy rounds and canons. All this makes for more enjoyable and varied music.

Take the old round, "Row, Row, Row Your Boat." The class has learned it thoroughly and can sing in two groups. Now they want to try some instrumental accompaniment. (Once children become familiar with the sound of instruments while singing, they want to use them at every opportunity.) Here is an arrangement one third year group worked out by the trial and error method:

1—The round is sung in two parts. (Very few eight-year-olds can handle a three-part round.)

2—Marge plays the "C" chord on the Autoharp on the first beat of each measure. This helps accent the beat of a melody that requires little accent but needs *some*. Only once does Marge have to change chords. On the word "Life" of "Life is but a dream" she plays the "G7" chord and on the word "dream" she is back to the familiar "C" chord again. Marge manages this very well and her class finds the effect pleasing. (She is teaching it to Kenny.)

3—Jim, Bobby and Marian use three bars of the resonator bells (C, E, G) to play the "C" chord. Since they found it crowded to stand together, they took one bar each to their seats and now play in comfort.

4—The drum and tambourine were immediately rejected for this gentle little song, but three children play triangles accenting the first beat of each measure. They share the honors with others from time to time.

5—Mrs. Hudson, the teacher, was the original director; however, she has trained Fred and Grace to act as assistants. They in turn are training two more classmates.

6—Alfred, who is a poor singer and hasn't a very well developed sense of rhythm, is right up there when it comes to mechanical things. He has made several tape recordings of the joint effort and the class selected the best of them to be played at a parents' meeting in the near future.

Third and fourth graders enjoy special effects

As you read earlier, third and fourth graders are ready to move out into the world and are increasingly interested in people who live in other environments. There is still the interest in firemen, trucks and buses (we never quite outgrow that), but eight- and nine-year-olds are curious about people of whom they read but rarely see in real life —the Indian sheepherder of the Southwest, the cowboy and his pony on a dusty trail, Latin-Americans who live in such a different climate and speak a different language. It is a curious age, eight or nine, and a child at this time is continually making great discoveries. His ear is keener and he wants to know, for example, why an Indian song sounds the way it does. It's pleasing and he likes it, but now he wants to know the why and how of everything.

Pentatonic music: The pentatonic scale consists of five notes— C, D, F, G, A or C sharp, D sharp, F sharp, G sharp, A sharp (the five black keys of the piano). Music using this scale has a definitely different sound to Western ears but is typical of American Indian songs as well as those of most Asiatic lands. It demands our attention and we find it appealing and, in some way, satisfying. We will discover, when we discuss creative music, that children enjoy using the pentatonic effect in songs they compose—often prefer it to "our" scale.

Let's see what Class 4–2 did for instrumental "effects" when they learned "Shepherd Boy at Night." There was a general discussion of the suitability of various instruments—could a drum be used in a song that is supposed to be sung "Gently"—how could they show the twinkling of desert stars (this knowledge gained from a story about the Southwest)—wouldn't Running Deer like to have a flute for company? (The boys said they'd rather have a dog, but the song didn't mention such a companion.)

This is what 4–2 agreed upon for orchestration:

   1—Two small drums with sticks wrapped in soft baby socks and played right through the entire song—two beats to a measure.
   2—"C" chord struck on Autoharp and piano *very gently* on the *first* beat of each measure right through the song.
   3—To show the twinkling of desert stars three children would strike triangles on each beat of lines three and four:

^ ^ ^ ^ ^   ^   ^ ^ ^   ^ ^ ^ ^ ^ ^
(Stars in desert sky shine bright, Stay nearby 'til day.)

Shepherd Boy at Night

4—The Tonette Study Group—which several class members hoped to join—had not been started for the fall term. Feeling a flute effect would be pleasing, Peter persuaded his sister in fifth grade to help out temporarily. She was asked to play the melody as the class sang and played "Shepherd Boy at Night."

5—(a) Class sings the song through once, without accompaniment, then (b) the orchestra plays it with flute carrying the melody, then (c) all together.

So, even though the song is short, it became quite a production when heard three times in an interesting variety of ways and was worthy of recording on tape.

Instruments you need in your classroom

Ideally, each classroom should have a variety of simple instruments —and a few good, factory-built ones—that can be used when needed, at any time of the school day. Too often we must share them with other classes and they're not available when we want them. This is frustrating and discouraging. With planning, much of this can be avoided, but it means getting other teachers to see the importance of planning their music lessons so enough shared instruments are available when needed. It's money, again, and there's never enough when it comes to music. Could it possibly be that, in this day and age, educators still (secretly) think of instruments as unessential frills—something slightly frivolous —one hundred years after we thought we had won them over?

Look at this list compiled by O. M. Hartsell of the University of Arizona in the bulletin "Teaching Music in the Elementary School: Opinion and Comment":[1]

"drums (at least one drum, and where possible, two or more of contrasting size), rhythm sticks, triangles, sandblocks, coconut shells, sleigh bells, tambourines, resonator bells, cymbals, gong, maracas, Quiro (gourd rasp), castanets, finger cymbals."

Professor Hartsell stresses the importance of each class having its own equipment "in the classroom on a permanent basis" and the need for a piano or an Autoharp "as some means of producing accurate pitch . . ."

This report is based upon questions asked *by teachers* in regard to music education in the classroom. Its purpose is to bring practical help to people concerned with the problem.

[1] Published in 1963 by the Association for Supervision and Curriculum Development, NEA, 1201 Sixteenth St., NW, Washington, D.C. 20036.

Interesting, useful instruments you can make

A teacher does not have to be completely dependent on the generosity of the local school board—or whoever holds the purse strings. There are many simple, homemade instruments that you and the children (depending on their age and ability) can make for yourselves. When children are young, they're not too much help in making an instrument but they can—and love to—dig up material for you if they know what to look for.

My father was brought up in a Canadian seaport city. There was no money for frills, no money to indulge any interest the children might have in music. Whatever the brothers and sisters wanted, other than bare necessities, they had to find or devise. Of course there was singing, but when it came to owning an instrument to make that singing more exciting, the children were on their own.

On the rare occasions when there was meat for dinner instead of the omnipresent fish, every bone was saved and jealously guarded. When the meat happened to be short ribs or spare ribs, it was an event—as much because of the bones as the meat. First, every speck of meat was picked from the bones which were subsequently scrubbed with soap and water and strung along the back of the wood stove to dry. If these bones were in the way of my busy grandmother she never said so. Every day the children inspected their treasure hoard to see if it was ready for the great concert.

When the time was ripe—and the bones too—chairs were arranged in a half-circle in the big, warm kitchen. Grandfather (grumbling about children's nonsense) was seated first, then Mother, Father, Uncle George and any assorted relatives who happened to be around. The children trooped in, led by Minnie who was the director. Each child held a pair of dry bones and two chair rungs salvaged from the neighbors. Baby Victoria struggled in last with a pair of pot covers.

Howard took up his position by the drum (Mother's wash boiler played with two padded chair rungs), and "God Save the King" was announced formally by the director. All stood and sang and the anthem ended with a flourish of the drum.

In the program that followed Minnie announced each number and even the youngest musician knew when to use the bones and when to use the chair rungs—they had never heard of "rhythm sticks."

It was wonderful fun and the children had the experience of working as a group to achieve something they never would have known if they had not planned every detail—used their ingenuity to get something they wanted.

Your first graders will gladly save bones, bring chair rungs, old pot-covers. If the idea of bones and chair rungs makes you uncomfortable, such rhythm instruments can be made of new material at little cost. You can buy it and, if you're unhandy with saw and paint and sand-paper, ask that kind shop teacher if he'll get his boys to do the work.

Let's look at the making of some simple instruments. See first what material is needed; then decide if your children are old enough to help. Don't expect the perfection of professionally made instruments—that's not the point. The experience of a class do-it-yourself project is what matters. The children will remember it long after they have gone to higher grades.

1—*Rhythm sticks*. Doweling is bought in lengths of a yard or more. Get it ⅜ to ⅝ inches in thickness, cut it into 12-inch lengths, sand-paper the rough ends and you have some nearly perfect rhythm sticks, light enough for small hands.

Remembering the age and ability of your grade, consider the pos-sibility of painting and decorating the sticks. Several pairs are needed so each child has a chance to become familiar with them.

2—*Claves*. Not for the youngest but fine for fifth and sixth grade boys and girls (who will probably want to give them the Spanish pronunciation "CLAH′vehs"). Ask for one-inch doweling—hard wood if possible—and cut into *8-inch* lengths. Caribbean in origin, claves are used to accent the rhythm of the rumba.

Hold one in the left hand and hit it with the clave in the right hand. If you have calypso records, see how well the accompaniment of claves fits the rhythm.

Stain the sticks dark and use your imagination when you paint designs in brilliant colors.

3—*Rhythm blocks*. Two identical squares of wood about 3″ by 3″ or 4″ by 4″ (but no larger) and less than an inch in thickness. Screw dime store pot-cover handles to blocks or nail on small wooden blocks one inch square and sandpaper all corners. Decorate as your heart desires. These blocks are struck together.

4—*Sand blocks*. Made like rhythm blocks with sandpaper glued or tacked on. Excellent for that "swish-swish" effect.

5—*Triangle*. Nothing can truly take the place of the delicate little instrument found in orchestras, but your children will get a lot of mileage from a piece of straight metal tubing suspended from a string and struck with a smaller piece of metal. Experiment with several to discover the best sound.

Try a wire coat hanger, held by its hook and tapped with a nail. Try several for some have a better sound than others. See what can be done with a well-scrubbed horseshoe, too.

6—*Cymbals*. Hard to beat a good pot cover or two; the handles are already in place. Strike them a glancing blow, either together or singly, hitting one with a rhythm stick. The cymbals player must have a good sense of rhythm, for if he comes in at the wrong time the whole effect is lost.

7—And as for a *gong,* the best one we ever had was a lucky accident. Linda ran into a metal table used to hold books and magazines. She was so annoyed that she kicked the fallen table. There was our gong! Only we didn't kick it to make the sound—we put a sock over a rhythm stick and used that for a mallet.

8—*Tambourines*. In lower grades try stapling several paper plates together for durability and sewing or stapling little dime-store bells around the edge. In this way you can make as many as you wish so each child becomes familiar with the way in which a tambourine is played. The instrument is decorated as gaily as the owner wishes— and be sure to add bright streamers of ribbon. If the exchequer is in bad shape, use narrow strips of crepe paper.

Class 2–2 made so many tambourines—and they were so appealingly pretty—that their teacher formed a "tambourine band" and had great success in teaching rhythms. The youngsters accompanied their own singing, made up little dances, beating the rhythm with tambourines and even played them with records.

I have seen some colorful Pan-American programs presented by sixth graders in which the dancers used the above type of tambourine. Sub-teeners seem to enjoy decorating and using these "homemade" instruments as much as their little brothers and sisters do.

9—*Drums*. Almost *anything* can be used to "drum out" a rhythm. It's fine to own a well-made drum, but if there are only one or two in a classroom few children get to know much about the instrument.

Since time began, fingers and fists and sticks have been used to drum on things—hollow logs, stretched animal skins or parchment. Even upturned baskets, pails and bowls have satisfied that inborn urge to pound out a rhythm for ceremonies or dancing. Don't deprive your youngsters of the great pleasure of drumming, just because fancy drums are out of the question. Here is an opportunity to experiment with ideas and see what the class can devise for drum substitutes.

Start simply, using the trial and error method. If you are *sure*

Don's idea will not work, let him try it anyway. He'll learn more science experimenting to find a substitute for a drum than you imagine and he'll know and remember what did *not* work and *why*. From fourth grade on, see that each child keeps an account of his own experiments in making drums—what worked and what did not and *why*. In lower grades discuss the progress made and keep the comments, pro and con, on the bulletin board for reference.

Try coffee cans—the one pound or the two pound size—the kind with the tight-fitting plastic top. They're easy to obtain which gives each child the chance to experiment:

a) Drum on the plastic top with fingers, pencil, spoon. How does it sound half-full of water? Is the sound improved or impaired if small holes are poked in the top?

b) Use two coffee cans held between the knees like bongo drums.

c) Strike two coffee cans together—plastic top against plastic top —metal bottom against metal bottom—plastic top against metal bottom.

d) What works best? Can you think of another way to experiment with these cans? Try decorating the best of them.

A slightly more difficult drum substitute

(And slightly more difficult to obtain.) If you or one of the children manages to get an old wooden salad bowl, one that Mother does not expect to be returned, a fine drum for class use can be made with some planning and care. The reason Mother won't get it back is that our friend the shop teacher will be asked to drill three holes for our fingers in the bottom of the bowl. These holes will (*a*) improve the sound and (*b*) make it easier to hold.

Better decorate the bowl before putting on the drum head. Cut oilcloth in a circle two inches larger than the top of the bowl and, with a friend to hold it tightly, hammer in tacks—first one tack in front and then one opposite it, alternately, until you have the oilcloth *very* tightly stretched across the top.

Experiment with a variety of beaters beginning with fingers, palms, pencils—see what gives the best beat.

A valuable book for your library

There is an interesting and useful book on the subject of making your own instruments written by Muriel Mandell and Robert E. Wood, published (1968) by Sterling Publishing Co., Inc., 419 Park Ave.

South, New York 10016. Its title is *Make Your Own Musical Instruments*. The authors go from the simple, better-known instruments to complicated drums using skin and drums made from fibre pipe and stove pipe. They discuss stringed instruments that children can make, from a simple wishbone harp to a more involved box banjo. There are illustrations throughout and explicit directions.

The above "salad bowl drum" is one of the suggestions to be found in the book and there are many more you will want to try as your children become involved in the idea of "do-it-yourself."

Billy experiments with coffee cans and cheese boxes

Sometimes a child comes to his teacher with an experiment carried out privately, on his own time—one that he wants to share with the class.

Billy attends a school that has a fine band and chorus. The teachers in charge of these groups do a remarkable job when one realizes that most of the children are under twelve. A good singing program is encouraged in the classrooms—but there music seems to stop. Everything is neat, pleasant, uncluttered; experimentation is seldom neat and therefore Billy's school has little of it.

It was near the end of summer vacation and Billy had just turned ten. You know how it is when vacation has become boring and yet you don't want school to begin. Children like to just "mess around" with nothing in particular.

Billy's Mom sent him to the back yard with directions to clean out the tool shed and that is where his adventure began. His younger brother, Johnny, age five, is an inveterate saver of junk and our hero found plenty of evidence of this habit in and around the tool shed. Frozen orange juice "cans"—the paper kind that have nice, neat tops and bottoms—were arranged along a shelf, some partly filled with gravel, pebbles and—Heaven knows how Johnny found it—rice! There were coffee cans with fine, tight-fitting plastic tops, partly filled with the same materials and small circular cheese boxes with almost perfect cardboard tops.

Billy was in no hurry and more than willing to have his attention distracted from the job. He shook one of the orange juice cans absentmindedly—hum! Not bad. He tried another—better. With one in each hand he took a few rumba steps learned in Mr. Thomas' gym class. Wow! This is what they should have used at the Spring Festival instead of just dancing to a record. The kids would like this.

Forgetting about his mother's displeasure when she would find him missing and the job neglected, he hot-footed it across the street to see if Dennis was home. He was and soon two youngsters were performing some of Mr. Thomas' dance steps much more energetically than in the confines of a gym. The boys tried the combination of rice in cheese boxes, rice in orange juice cans and in coffee cans, switching to gravel and then to pebbles. Some were good, some poor, some had a real beat, some a pleasant, soft "swish." One of the more satisfying sounds came from a flat little cheese box that Johnny had filled with pop-bottle caps. "Man. Just like chopper blades!" agreed Billy and Dennis. (To the uninitiated, a "chopper" is a helicopter.)

When Billy met his new teacher he lost no time telling about the experiments. A perfect opportunity presented itself when Mrs. Golden asked if anyone wanted to tell the class about something exciting that had happened during vacation. To Mrs. Golden's credit she was able to recognize a good thing when she saw it and immediately appointed Billy to the chairmanship of a science committee whose first challenge was to prepare, explain and put into use an exhibit of rhythm making instruments.

Fifth and sixth graders have more dexterity

By the time children reach the age of ten or eleven their muscles are better able to work with either a small or a large object. There is an improved sense of timing, a greater desire for perfection and a growing realization of the pleasures and responsibilities of teamwork.

All this should lead to a much improved music program. Perhaps several class members are learning to play an orchestral or band instrument under the guidance of a private teacher or with a special group in school. You may find two children who can accompany the singing with treble and bass chords on the piano. If there is a budding violinist, ask him to play the descants shown in music readers. We can hope that someone is studying guitar or uke, for these will add much to the beauty of Latin-American and Hawaiian music. The boy who is studying drums in the school band can teach a new beat to his classmates. You can change that old "1-2-1-2-3" to a more exciting, syncopated beat to use with a calypso or perhaps a rumba—or a beat that accompanies a spiritual—or a work song from the Caribbean.

Children who are not taking special lessons (probably the majority of the class) are able to contribute their share with their increased ability to make finer rhythm instruments. We still need the

"CLAH'vehs," maracas (or rattle) types, substitutes for triangles; and now castanets play their part to make dance music more interesting as eleven-year-old hands are more adept at managing them.

If you have one or two boys (or girls) who are "good at making things" challenge them with a "washtub bass" and, if they meet that challenge, a "My-olin." (See Mandell and Wood's *Make Your Own Musical Instruments.*)

Plan ahead, don't expect perfection overnight, use any abilities your class can contribute—some special, some limited. Even if you lack musical training or experience, it is possible for your class to use a variety of simple instruments, to give each child a chance to offer something, to have enjoyable music lessons, to prepare special programs to present to others, and to make music alive and challenging.

Something unusual to look into

Completely by chance I came across a newspaper clipping about a Miss Margaret Galloway, born in Britain but now connected with the music program of the University of Toronto's Institute of Child Study.

Miss Galloway and her brother, an engineer, design and make educational instruments for children. To quote Miss Galloway, "Children develop a better taste for music if they can provide their own accompaniment for songs and their own music—but you've got to start off with simple instruments."

The new company calls itself "Educational Musical Instruments" or "E.M.I." Each instrument is made individually by hand from the finest available materials and "robust enough for hard use in classroom or home." These are traditional instruments—an Octave Psaltery to be plucked with finger, quill or plectrum; a Two Octave Zither—also to be plucked; a Nordic Lyre and a Chordal Dulcimer. The Bowed Psaltery is a more modern instrument, first developed in Germany and "designed to introduce the child to the family of bowed instruments."

Recently the "E.M.I." Company has introduced another stringed instrument, an Appalachian Dulcimer with three strings. Also new are simplified pipes of varied pitch with only one note and there are three sizes of shepherd pipes.

Sound intriguing? There is a growing demand from schools in the United States for these unusual instruments. Why not send for Miss Galloway's circular so you can discuss with your music supervisor or principal the possibility of adding something new and practical to your music program?

Write to:

> Educational Musical Instruments
> 46 Shilton Road
> Agincourt, Ontario
> Canada

Ask for the illustrated brochure and price list.

INSTRUMENTS ADD GREATLY TO THE ENJOYMENT OF CLASSROOM MUSIC

1—It has taken many years for educators to realize that every child should have the chance to use instruments in the classroom.

2—Often we find that a child who cannot contribute much to the singing is quite capable of using a simple instrument to accompany his classmates.

3—Young children enjoy playing an instrument that encourages large, free movements of hand and arm such as a drum, cymbals, a triangle or rhythm sticks.

4—Start simply. If children have difficulty keeping the rhythm with a drum, for example, practice *clapping* the rhythm.

5—Never assume that *any* child knows how to use *any* instrument. Add one instrument at a time and let the boys and girls experiment with its use. Familiarity with a drum or any other instrument is important.

6—Encourage children to help each other learn how to use rhythm sticks, triangles, tambourines and so forth. One child is very often successful in teaching a skill to another.

7—The Autoharp is a perfect accompaniment for children's songs. In first grade the teacher uses it but encourages those who are interested to "help" her by strumming the strings as she presses the button for a chord.

8—Resonator bells may be used in second grade to play simple three-toned songs. As children reach higher grades they enjoy playing duets in "thirds."

9—Experience with resonator bells paves the way for simple piano accompaniments since the bars of the resonator bells are in the same relative position as the keys of the piano.

10—Instruments are helpful in teaching children to *accent the beat*. The addition of a drum, triangle or rhythm sticks on the *first* beat of a song in 3/4 time—or on the *first* and *third* beats of a song in 4/4 time —makes singing more interesting.

11—If children have the chance to experiment with a variety of instruments they become more discerning in their choice of the right instrument for the desired effect.

12—Music educators deplore the scarcity of good instruments in classrooms. It's usually a question of lack of available funds.

13—Consider the possibility of *making* some simple rhythm instruments so all your children may enjoy them. Scrap material can be salvaged from garage and kitchen or new material can be bought at small cost. Ingenuity plays a large part in the success of such a project.

14—Children are proud of their simple "homemade" rhythm instruments and take great delight in painting them and decorating them with bright colors.

15—Don't permit your rhythm band to be exploited for the entertainment of the neighborhood. Interclass concerts are fine and a good experience for all concerned.

Part Three

PUTTING MUSIC TO
WORK IN THE CLASSROOM

The children's background has now been taught but should be reviewed frequently and weak spots strengthened. Now you and the class can really *use* music as an integral part of the school day.

Let music waken the creativity that sleeps in all of us. Encourage children to write poems, create the music for them, compose new parts for songs and instrumental accompaniments, plan a fine assembly program.

Creativity in a permissive atmosphere is often wasted on trivia, but creativity within an atmosphere of understanding discipline gets results.

Help your children to appreciate the vital role of music in understanding others—a *must* in today's chaotic world.

chapter 7

Creative Music—More
Than Creating a Song

In any discussion of teaching music to children it is natural that creativity enters the picture frequently. We have read in previous chapters instances of creativity where children and teacher, working together with a common interest, produce surprising and satisfying results. There must be planning and guidance in creativity for, unless there is some discipline, creativity may get out of hand and our efforts are wasted.

When we hear the term "creativity in music" we picture someone sitting down and composing a song—but for the purposes of this chapter "creativity in music" means many other things as well.

It means selecting the right instruments to express the mood of a song. It means arranging a melody for part singing, making up simple orchestrations, composing descants and ostinatos, planning interclass visits or an assembly program—and it means composing a song, too.

All this may seem like a tall order for the children in your class but it's not. They can do it under your guidance and get a tremendous kick out of it.

Teachers ask, "Just what *is* creativity?" "How do we evoke it?"

"What kind of atmosphere encourages it?" "Isn't a permissive attitude essential if we want children to express themselves naturally?" "Can't I have a well-disciplined class and encourage creativity at the same time?"

Let's examine this subject of self-expression, spontaneity, creativity —call it what you will. Perhaps we can come up with the answers.

"What *is* creativity?"

Creativity, by its very nature, precludes a simple, pat definition. It may be that tiny touch of genius we discover now and then in ourselves which makes us feel so good. A homemaker who fears she's unappreciated and in a rut is inspired to try a daring combination of ingredients in the family's "taken for granted" Irish stew and wins their plaudits. "Oh, it's really nothing," she says, but suddenly her kitchen seems more important and she goes on to try a new pudding or plan a foreign meal as a surprise.

John Dewey says that every individual is in some way original and creative—it's part of a person's make-up—his individuality. He makes a most important point: *we must get rid of what stifles creativity for if we can do that we will find an opportunity to express ourselves constructively.* Dewey adds that neither the extent nor the area of one's creative efforts is as important as its quality and intensity.

We know, as adults, the countless ways in which our own spontaneity, our own desires for self-expression are suppressed. Perhaps through the years we have, from necessity or expediency, permitted it to happen. Can't we see to it that children in our care have opportunities to be themselves—to let that occasional spark of originality shine when it's ready? Do you remember the satisfaction and warmth and renewal of faith in yourself that a period of creativity brought to you?

An atmosphere conducive to creativity

Small children left to themselves to play make up their own little rhymes and songs. There is an unconsciousness of self as the tots pick up toys, talk and sing to them, carry on a conversation with a doll or favorite bunny, enjoy a world of their own, free from adult interference. Call the child away from this private world and suddenly the songs are gone and, more than likely, tears appear.

Why couldn't Mother leave him alone? Time for lunch? Mommy has to go shopping? Nap time? The world of necessities obtrudes. Creativity with its relaxed self-expression is thrust aside. That's life and, child or adult, we must face it. The child's busy mother certainly has to face it; his daddy, fighting traffic and competition ten hours a day, has to face it; big brother, worried about his Spanish mark, has to face it. When this child comes into our classroom, let's see if we cannot provide some "islands of refuge" during the school day—some periods of fun and relaxation when we all let down our hair and give creativity a chance to break through the barriers that life imposes upon it.

Sometimes these moments are unplanned—just happen—and present an ideal situation to an alert teacher. Miss Jacobs, for example, although timid about teaching music, saw her opportunity to interest a class that seemed cold to the whole idea of classroom music and guided her children through a series of creative music experiences. We found another group making up their own dance steps to the old favorite, "Oh, Susanna!" Other children experimented with instruments such as drums, rhythm sticks, bells, Autoharp and cymbals to find the desired combination of sounds to make a perfect accompaniment for a song.

In each case there was something going on that *created the interest first*. This interest grew as the children offered original ideas about mood, tempo, dynamics and rhythm. The class considered each suggestion, discussed it, experimented with it. The end product was a satisfying piece of work—each one contributing something of himself—and all taking pride in their creation. No boisterous adult came bursting into the room with fake enthusiasm announcing, "Today we're going to write a song!" But a sympathetic adult was there to capitalize on the children's natural creativity as it arose.

Does a permissive attitude encourage creativity?

That depends entirely on the individual teacher's interpretation of "permissive." While "permissiveness" was the "in" thing sometime back, we have now come to frown upon it as a sign of weakness in adults that won little thanks from our children and more often earned their contempt. Permissiveness meant a complete lack of discipline and without discipline there's little satisfaction in anything.

Have you ever tried to teach math to an undisciplined class? Have you tried to present an art lesson to such a group? Creativity has little chance to flourish under an iron hand, but the child whose parent and teacher have found the happy medium is lucky indeed.

An "old-timer's" reaction to permissiveness

Mrs. Stewart, an "old-timer" who has retired but likes to sub now and then, had an experience she later described as traumatic when she innocently accepted a substitution assignment during Open School Week.

The phone rang early one dark November morning.

"Can you help us out today?" asked the school secretary. In an anxious tone she explained to Mrs. Stewart that Miss Collins had been stricken with a bug and was frantic about her class. The children were supposed to be unusually bright and were planning a special show of their own for visiting parents that very afternoon. If Mrs. Stewart could help them today, the school would be eternally grateful.

"Why not?" said the good lady. "Parents can't frighten me at this stage of the game. I'll be there in an hour."

There was an anguished cry when Mrs. Stewart entered the room. Their teacher! Where was she? Excited groups milled about the room or talked shrilly in corners. Above the ensuing bedlam Mrs. Stewart could hear shrieks and bits of loud conversation:

"My mother will *die* if she can't talk to Miss Collins!"

"Your *mother* will die! *I'll* die if we can't find the record for my dance!"

"Everything's ruined! Why'd she have to get sick *TODAY?*"

After Mrs. Stewart's first shock of disbelief had passed, she rapped sharply for order. Nothing happened—absolutely nothing. Those not engaged in exaggerated conversation scurried about trying to open closets that might conceal some costume or gadget needed for the entertainment.

"Go to your seats at once!" ordered Mrs. Stewart.

"We don't have any seats," said one youngster in a supercilious manner. "We sit where we want to. Miss Collins says seats are old-fashioned. She says she doesn't want our initiative suppressed."

"I'll suppress your initiative," said Mrs. Stewart. "Every child in this room go to a seat before I count to three."

They sat. It was a very quiet room.

When the substitute's Scotch blood had simmered down to a point below boiling she talked quietly to the class. (How ridiculous to allow herself to become so annoyed. She must be losing her grip.) She explained to the children that their teacher was ill and she had come to help out. Now, if everyone cooperated they would get along just fine.

If Mrs. Stewart asked the class to do a certain thing they must co-operate for the good of all.

Heads nodded agreement. (See? They were just kids and needed a little firmness.)

The morning proceeded fairly well. Mrs. Stewart kept the children busy for a while with written assignments. She wanted an opportunity to get the feel of the room and the group that occupied it. There must be some central theme, some thread of plan and purpose running through all this . . . this . . .—what word would fit it?

Still puzzled, Mrs. Stewart checked the assignments and answered the rather fresh objections from the class while commenting dryly on their general lack of practical knowledge. When she attempted to explain why some practical knowledge of such details as fractions and punctuation was a necessity, the children displayed little interest and there was a general exodus from seats to the several corners of the room.

Kenneth, the class president, asked for rehearsal time to prepare for the afternoon festivities. That was all right with the teacher. She was curious about it anyway. Much to her surprise, it went well. Such things as choral speaking and original poetry made sense to her. Elaine was the capable mistress of ceremonies, introducing each number graciously.

"Well," said Mrs. Stewart, "I want to congratulate you. Your parents will enjoy this entertainment, I'm sure, and they'll be proud of you."

Said Elaine, "But the best part comes last. Miss Collins has planned a surprise for the closing number. She has a record put away in the top drawer of her desk and she's the only one who knows what it is. While it's being played each one of us will do whatever the record tells us to do. That should be fun!"

Somewhere in the back of Mrs. Stewart's mind a warning bell rang, but she ignored it, saying to herself, "I will not be an old fogey—not today, anyway. I'll go along with them and maybe I'll learn something."

Creativity without purpose or direction

During the noon hour—which Mrs. Stewart decided to spend in the classroom, she took the record from the top drawer of Miss Collins' desk.

"Don't know if this is cricket," she mused, "but I *have* to know what it is and I'd better try out the record player."

"John Alden Carpenter—'Adventures in a Perambulator'—hm-m. Sounds intriguing. A suite for orchestra—hm-m. According to the label here, the baby encounters a policeman, a hand-organ, sees a lake, hears some dogs—and the last part is called 'Dreams.' Sounds as though it might be delightful. Wonder how these youngsters will react?"

The afternoon started beautifully. Miss Collins had surely trained the young host and hostess in their jobs, for each parent was smilingly shown to a seat (the children weren't using them anyway) and Elaine introduced Mrs. Stewart to the visitors. ("I never had much luck with that," thought the veteran teacher. "Could be Miss Collins knows something after all.")

Choral speaking, original poems and limericks, a tap dance, a flute solo—this was *too* good. But then, they didn't know fractions, did they? Nor punctuation and heaven knows what else. Many thoughts went swiftly through Mrs. Stewart's mind as she sat and listened— more like a guest than a substitute teacher.

Now it was time for the *pièce de résistance,* the great experiment. Elaine explained to the parents what was about to happen.

"Sometimes," said Elaine, "Miss Collins plays a record that we know and we paint or draw while we listen to the music. At other times she takes a record we never heard and lets us paint or dance or do any- thing that comes to mind—anything the music tells us to do. Today Mrs. Stewart has a record that Miss Collins selected, but we don't know what it is. Would you like to see what happens?"

Most of the parents smiled agreeably. Mrs. Stewart's years of ex- perience said something was amiss but—on with the show! Without comment she placed the record on the machine and started it. She felt there should be at least some introduction—the name of the composer or perhaps the names of the movements of the suite. But she did what Miss Collins wanted and resumed her sitting position.

"Adventures in a Perambulator" started peacefully. The children evidently knew how to listen to music—if not to a teacher. After a while one child and then another went to the board and drew seem- ingly aimless designs. A few helped themselves to paper and paints or crayons, found a place to sit and started work.

When the hand-organ played, two boys became organ-grinder and monkey, much to the amusement of the spectators. One of the girls at the board drew into her design what everyone felt must surely be a monkey.

Attention and interest lagged during the "Lake" movement and Mrs. Stewart devoutly wished she had the nerve to stop the whole business.

But when "The Dogs" started, things changed rapidly—for the worse. First it was the yapping effect created by the orchestra. Quite naturally, one child, then two, began yapping and Mrs. Stewart was about to check their enthusiasm when one of the "dogs" decided to snap at some ankles while creeping around on all fours. The situation was saved from complete disintegration by a sudden change in the music to "Where, Oh Where Has My Little Dog Gone?" Just as the children attempted to sing, the tune suddenly changed to "Ach Du Lieber Augustin" and there was a little confusion.

"Dreams" started softly and Miss Collins' children acted as though they had finished with creativity and were ready for a change of activity. "And about time," sighed Mrs. Stewart—but she reckoned without Freddie. He rose slowly from the floor where he had been relaxing and, as in a trance, raised his arms and swirling, bowing and kicking his heels made his awkward way past parents, chairs and classmates toward the front of the crowded classroom.

The music stopped—but not Freddie. Parents cast nervous looks at each other and at the poor substitute teacher. The children began to laugh as though they had suddenly joined the ranks of more ordinary humans.

"Freddie!" said Mrs. Stewart sharply. Nothing happened.

"Freddie! Stop!" she called again. His classmates were in hysterics.

Mrs. Stewart rose, grabbed Freddie by the shoulder and sat him down, none too gently. "That's enough."

One embarrassed parent after another left the classroom, murmuring nothings like "Thank you," "Lovely entertainment," "Must get my little girl from the kindergarten."

In the few minutes remaining before dismissal, this was one of the quietest rooms you've ever seen. Mrs. Stewart sat at her desk, weak as a kitten. The children sat—they must have been exhausted. There was no conversation. The teacher could think of nothing to say to the children. They, in turn, seemed more than willing to wait quietly for the end of the day. Perhaps they were just grateful that Mrs. Stewart had been rendered speechless. Freddie showed no resentment—nor did he show the least embarrassment.

This "happening" leaves some unanswered questions:

1—Is Miss Collins being fair to her class?
    a) The children are relaxed, exploring new areas, free from pressures, enjoying what they are doing.
    b) The children are free to move about at will, to consult each other at any time, to ignore the wishes of the person

responsible for their well-being, to consider their own project of the moment more important than anything else.

c) What happens when these children leave Miss Collins—as they must—and go to another teacher who believes that she or he is expected to teach what the curriculum calls for; that the world is not going to put up with such lack of competence in practical matters?

2—Was Mrs. Stewart too strict?

a) When the substitute teacher recovered from the first shock, she really tried to go along with the day as it had been planned—admitted that Miss Collins might have some good ideas—was willing to learn something new.

b) When things got completely out of hand, she reacted as a teacher should (and as most parents do if they are not afraid of their offspring).

c) Mrs. Stewart was never an iron-rod disciplinarian. Her many classes through the years liked her for her insistence on acceptable behavior and fairness to all.

3—Is "freedom within discipline" an impossible goal?

a) The majority of the teachers with whom I have worked seem to have reached some fairly happy medium between complete freedom of choice in the classroom and teacher domination. To expect every period of the school day to be creative is nonsense. But if a teacher talks too much, directs each movement, expects small humans to respond like automatons, it is not only unrealistic but cruel.

b) It takes a strong teacher to maintain an even balance all day, every day, and few of us are that strong. But if we laugh and talk and sing with our children, scold when they need it, we can make an occasional mistake—even to being unwise in a weak moment—and they'll like us better for proving we're human. When teacher and children understand and really like each other, we have the perfect background for creativity—an "atmosphere conducive to it."

Musical creativity in first grade

Miss Linden was showing her first graders how to breathe properly while singing. Of course they didn't know they were being taught to breathe properly—the class thought it was just a game. (A very helpful trick in any grade.)

First Miss Linden asked her children to sing [musical notation: loo - loo] while
she counted 1-2-3-4 with her hands. (See Chapter 2.) The idea was to use only *one* breath for the *four* counts. (Small children tend to breathe in the middle of a word.)

After several tries Janie said, "I think 'loo-loo' sounds silly, Miss Linden. Can't we sing real words?"

"That's a good idea, Janie," said her teacher. "Do you have some better words for the song?"

Without hesitation Janie sang, right on pitch,

[musical notation: Hel - lo   Good - bye]

beating 1-2-3-4 in imitation of her teacher.

"Oh, that's good, Janie," said her best friend, Edie.

"You don't say 'Hello' and then 'Goodbye' right after it," pointed out Peter. "You should say 'Hello' to somebody."

"Somebody—who?" asked Ronnie.

"Well, today on the way to school I said 'Hello' to a robin," admitted Peter. His classmates giggled.

Miss Linden defended Peter. "I like that," she said. "Birds usually stay around places where people are kind to them. Do you know why you saw a robin this morning, Peter?"

"Because summer's coming!" interrupted Charles who liked to steal other people's thunder. "Listen!"

[musical notation: Sum - mer's   com - ing]

Miss Linden started to reprimand Charles; then, realizing she might have something worthwhile here, decided the rebuke could wait.

"Let's try that," she said. "Take your hands and hold them high like I'm doing and then bring them down while we count. Janie, Edie, Peter, Charles, you come up here and help me."

With all that assistance Miss Linden soon had most of the children singing the phrase, "Hel-lo—Ro-bin" beating 1-2-3-4. "The breath control can wait," thought the teacher. "This is too good to interrupt."

It wasn't hard to add Charles' contribution—in fact, he insisted upon it—and now the class had a tiny song of their own. Miss Linden drew a "picture" of the song on the board while the children sang and beat time.

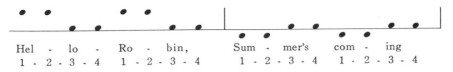

Hel - lo - Ro - bin,   Sum - mer's   com - ing
1 - 2 - 3 - 4   1 - 2 - 3 - 4   1 - 2 - 3 - 4   1 - 2 - 3 - 4

When Linda and Lennie, the twins, returned after lunch, they raced each other to the teacher shouting breathlessly, "Miss Linden! Miss Linden! When we walked to school with our mother we saw a redwing, a redwing! Our mother said it was a redwing! And it whistled and scolded. Our mother says it has a nest and that's why it scolded. Can't we have a redwing, a redwing in our song? Let's have a redwing in our song."

When the other children saw a picture of the red-winged blackbird they agreed he, too, should be in the new song—"He's so pretty!" and now the song is twice as long.

Greetings To The Birds

By Class 1-3

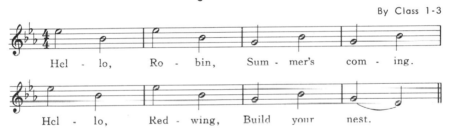

Hel - lo,   Ro - bin,   Sum - mer's   com - ing.

Hel - lo,   Red - wing,   Build   your   nest.

"Greetings to the Birds" at first started on "C" which was high "Do." Miss Linden raised the pitch so that high "Do" was now "E flat." It made the song brighter. You will notice that the ending is a bit different. That's because the children were dissatisfied with the song ending on an "up" note and tried several endings. This was their favorite.

The staff will not be used in singing "Greetings" at present. When Miss Linden's class has sung many songs, drawn "pictures" of them in the air, composed more melodies, then it will be time enough to take a look at the staff.

Choral speaking paves the way for creating melodies

It's a well-known fact that choral speaking gives the individuals in a group a sense of belonging, a sense of security. The timidities that plague many children vanish when they join their voices in a successful production. The feeling that "We did this" and "My group did this" means so much to a child. His team, her friends—confidence is built, fears vanish, ideas can take root and flourish.

The rhythm, the accent, the mood of a choral speaking number carries over naturally to the creation of melodies to fit the words. Some poems almost set themselves to music and then there is the double pleasure of speaking the words and creating the music that will enhance them. It is not at all unusual for children of any age to sing as readily as they speak, so when the group plans such an activity—or when it "just happens," it should not surprise us.

Here are four poems, learned for choral speaking in grades 2 through 6, poems that developed naturally into songs because they had a rhythm that called for music, a mood that impressed the children (not all gay moods) and—most important of all—were favorites of the various groups. Three are by famous poets—one is anonymous.

1) Grade 2—*The Big Bass Drum* (Anonymous)

Oh! we can play on the violin,
And this is the way we do it;
Zum, zum, zin, says the violin,
Rub-a-dub, boom, goes the big bass drum.
And this is the way we do it.

> Oh! we can play on the little flute,
> And this is the way we do it;
> Tootle, toot, toot, says the little flute,
> Zum, zum, zin, goes the violin,
> Rub-a-dub, boom, goes the big bass drum.
> And this is the way we do it.

These children had pretended to play the bass drum, violin and flute in the choral speaking. Now that they had a song, the bass drum became a metal table and a padded drumstick; the violin, an elastic stretched on a ruler and played by a pencil (still an imitation) with a paper comb for the "zum, zum, zin" effect; the flute, a borrowed recorder played well enough to give everyone a thrill.

The repetition of lines in verses 2 and 3 gave the players momentary pause, but they soon conquered the problem.

2) Grade 3—*The Swing* by Robert Louis Stevenson (Music by 3–1)

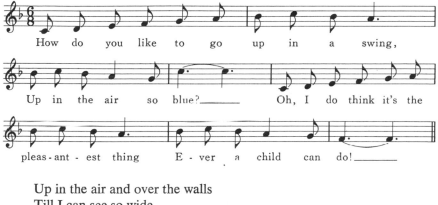

How do you like to go up in a swing,
Up in the air so blue?_____ Oh, I do think it's the
pleas-ant-est thing E-ver a child can do!_____

Up in the air and over the walls
Till I can see so wide,
Rivers and trees and cattle and all
Over the countryside—

Till I look down on the garden green,
Down on the roof so brown—
Up in the air I go flying again,
Up in the air and down!

The children seemed to have gotten the effect of the smooth rise and fall of the swing—something all of them had experienced frequently. They used the help of the ascending and descending scale to good advantage.

3) Grade 5—*A Bird Came Down the Walk* by Emily Dickinson (Music by 5–1)

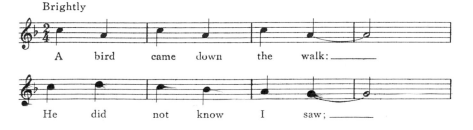

Brightly

A bird came down the walk:_____
He did not know I saw;_____

And then he drank a dew/From a convenient grass,
And then hopped sideways to the wall/To let a beetle pass.

This choral speaking number was great fun for everyone—after some of the girls conquered their first squeamishness. It was agreed that the mood should be essentially gay and that the rhythm of the music must suggest the pert, bright-eyed appearance of a bird.

4)   Grade 6—*My Heart Leaps Up* by William Wordsworth

(Music by 6–4)

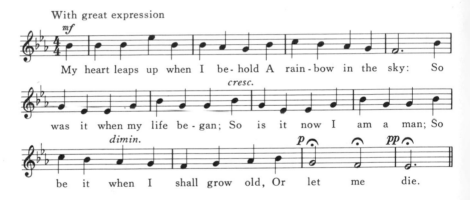

Here we have a short, beautiful poem by one of the masters. When it was presented to the class the teacher did not expect much reaction, thinking it possibly too mature for pre-teeners. He simply wanted the children to hear a tiny gem of literature.

To the teacher's surprise his sixth-graders wanted to talk about it. They understood that this is not a sad poem, for the thrill of seeing a rainbow dominates the theme. They felt, with Wordsworth, that if a person loses his ability to rejoice in the beauties of Nature, his life is empty.

The marks of expression in the music are almost identical with those developed in choral speaking. The children were much impressed when they realized how closely the music they created followed the inflection of the spoken words.

Class 5–4 plans an assembly program

Possibly no assembly program ever had a more peculiar beginning. It all began with the mispronunciation of the name "Cohan."

Mr. Webb asked Ted to do some research about the composer of "You're a Grand Old Flag" which the class was learning for the coming Flag Day celebration. Ted, who can spell anything, came to his teacher with a complaint about the encyclopedia.

"I've found a mistake in spelling in the encyclopedia," he told Mr. Webb with ill-concealed pleasure. "They've spelled 'Cohen' with an 'a.' First time *I* ever found a mistake in spelling in a book like this."

Ted was slightly crestfallen when his teacher assured him that "Cohen" and "Cohan" are two entirely different names, the latter being Irish.

As Ted continued his research he found himself becoming very much interested in the Cohan family—father, mother, sister Josie and George M.— who called themselves "The Four Cohans" and toured the country entertaining with songs and dances. As Ted reported on his findings, Mr. Webb could see (or do teachers *feel* these things?) that there was more than an average amount of interest in the Cohan family. Jerry Cohen started the ball rolling.

"I have an idea," he announced to the class. Jerry always had an idea and many of them were good, so his classmates waited with some anticipation.

"As long as we're planning 'You're a Grand Old Flag' for Flag Day, why don't we plan a whole Flag Day show? Now, wait a minute —I'm not finished . . ." (as he was interrupted by a flurry of hand-waving) "I think *I* should make the opening speech—who's got a better right to explain 'Cohen' and 'Cohan'?"

It was agreed that Jerry should introduce the program. He had a good voice, a sense of humor—so why not make him master of ceremonies?

It takes a great deal of research, planning and rehearsing to present a good assembly program. When you're studying a man who was much more than a "song and dance man"; one who wrote plays and acted in them; wrote the music for, and acted in, what was known as musical comedy a generation or two ago; was a producer of Broadway shows; was awarded the Congressional Medal of Honor, then you're taking on quite an assignment.

A question came up for discussion almost immediately. If this was to be called a Flag Day program, how well would Cohan's music fit it? Some children thought a Flag Day program should tell the story of the flag, show the proper ways to display it and how it grew from thirteen stars to its present number. The Cohan backers had their answers to that:

1—Use a good record of Sousa's "Stars and Stripes Forever" as the classes entered the assembly hall.

2—Follow this with the salute to the flag, complete with color guard.

3—Sing "The Star Spangled Banner."

4—Next, a script prepared by a group of four students telling about the flag and Flag Day.

5—Jerry would then take over the MC duties telling the assembled classes about the "Yankee Doodle Boy," born (he always claimed) on the Fourth of July. A small group—two or three at most—would assist Jerry with his script.

It wasn't difficult to persuade the rest of the class that the two ideas could be combined so that the flag was not slighted on its birthday and there would still be an exciting program to prepare and present.

Visits to libraries and music stores came next so all the material could be gathered. The Music Stores Committee returned with lists of records and a book of Cohan selections. Library committeemen returned with notebook pages full of facts about the Cohans and especially about George M.

Other problems had to be decided: there were Cohan songs like "Over There," "You're a Grand Old Flag," "Yankee Doodle Boy," all in the patriotic class. But the girls were very much in love with "Mary's a Grand Old Name," and "So Long, Mary." Everyone insisted on "Harrigan." Too much singing would bore the audience but what were the "producers" willing to leave out?

Committee chairmen met with Mr. Webb to plan a program that would (a) be practical to perform, (b) please and challenge the children who must prepare it and (c) be interesting and instructive to the spectators. The first five numbers previously suggested were kept intact. The following suggestions made by the committee were to be voted upon by the whole group:

1—"Over There" played softly as background music while Jerry introduced the program.

2—"Yankee Doodle Boy" sung by the class while George M., complete with straw hat and cane, soft-shoed up and down the stage.

3—One "Mary" song would be enough and the committee suggested "Mary's a Grand Old Name" with a recorded voice singing while several couples "strolled in the park" being very attentive to each other. Girls might wear big hats and carry parasols; boys, straw hats and canes.

4—"Harrigan" was to be the fun number. The Four Cohans, all wearing hats and carrying a cane or parasol, would dance in front of a large group of classmates who were to be singing "H—A—double R—I—G—A—N spells Harrigan"—just the chorus, but sung and danced twice.

Approval of the program was almost unanimous. Additional suggestions were made and the following added to the program:

1. Bert will perform with a drum-roll before the Flag Salute.

2. He and his brother, David—from sixth grade—will accompany the national anthem with drums—"Like the Marine Band on TV," Bert boasted.

3. Angela's banjo would be wonderful with "Harrigan." Would she practice? (She would.)

4. Experiment with an electric fan to see if it made the flag ripple in the breeze during the finale.

Could any experience be more creative than planning such a program? Here was a group of thirty, united in a common interest, planning, seeking, devising, using judgment, taking pride in a joint effort. Whether the program is musical in background or scientific or historical makes little difference. A group of children experiencing the warmth and good fellowship of a successful project will be so much richer for it.

Mr. Webb provided the "atmosphere conducive to creativity" without which there would have been little enthusiasm or success and, like a wise teacher, kept his finger on the class pulse. Yet he was able to prevent that sense of teacher domination so fatal to a child's initiative while still preventing the permissiveness under which everything goes to pieces.

"Composer of the Month" series

Mr. Barth's sixth graders study one composer a month as part of their musical experience. Each month a group of volunteers meets, decides on what composer it will report, hunts up stories, pictures and records, and plans a program to present to the class. Each child is expected to volunteer his services at least once, but sometimes there is a hesitant pupil who has to be teamed up with a more ambitious classmate.

The children in the group select their composer and then go to work on research and planning, presenting the program only when Mr. Barth has given his OK to the group's preparation and readiness to perform. Great emphasis is put upon thoroughness of preparation *and* originality of presentation.

The first group, for example, decided to study Mozart. As might be expected, the first group to volunteer was composed of children more musically gifted and more confident of their ability to do a thorough job. Peggy studies piano and so does Florence. Bernie learned to play a recorder in his previous class. Bob's parents have a fair-sized record library. The other two volunteers, Betty and Harry, like to plan things.

For a first attempt, they presented a program that had its flaws but was surprisingly well worked out, with a variety of Mozart recordings, from his "Turkish March" to selections from "The Magic Flute." There was even an original skit that showed the child, Mozart, at the court of Maria Theresa of Austria at the time of his meeting the Empress' little daughter, Marie Antoinette.

Another group, inspired by a film about the Berkshire Festival, decided to work on modern composers. Finding themselves swamped by too much material, they selected Aaron Copland for they liked his music about the United States, such as "Rodeo" and "Billy the Kid."

After several months had gone by (and every child had contributed something to the program), an idea popped up, seemingly from nowhere.

"Why can't we do something more with all this information we've been gathering?" asked Philip. "We've shared it with each other and have *pages* in our notebooks full of notes on composers and records. What happens now?"

Mr. Barth knew what he *hoped* would "happen now" but decided to sit back and see if the children came up with a worthwhile idea of their own.

"My friends in other classes don't know much about composers," said Shirley. "When we walk home together and I tell them what we're doing in music, they seem surprised."

"Why don't we write a book?" asked Tommy.

"How would all those kids use *one little book?*" said Frank. "It would just sit on a shelf and nobody would get to look at it."

Up bounced Elsie, both hands waving.

"Mr. Barth! Mr. Barth! I know!" she half shouted. "Are we allowed to use the public address system? We could broadcast our own music programs to the whole school. We could tell everyone at once what we've been doing."

The idea appealed to Elsie's classmates. If this could be worked out, it might be the ideal way to share their hard-won knowledge. Mr. Barth already was ticking off in his mind the problems these enthusiastic youngsters would have to solve.

After a good deal of discussion and a blackboard full of ideas, the children began to sort through the dozens of suggestions and questions. Mr. Barth told them to think about it overnight—"sleep on it," talk it over at home, think about the part each would like to play—announcers, performers, sound crew, publicity committee and so forth. Not one of them had realized the complexity of the job ahead. Not one of them wanted to back out.

The next day Mr. Barth's class went to work on their new project in earnest. Here's a partial list of plans laid out for this exciting, creative activity:

1—The class officers would arrange a meeting with the principal. With a prepared outline in their hands, they would tell him of their ideas and ask his permission to begin work. (This seemed a good starting point, for school equipment was to be used and most of the grades involved.) Naturally, everything planned had to wait for an official OK.

2—Everyone in the class was expected—and needed—to help out in some way. Besides the people who performed there were others just as important. (Where would radio and TV personalities be without whole crews of workers one never sees?)

3—Publicity men were needed to prepare posters for the halls so the programs would be well advertised.

4—Mr. Barth was chosen unanimously to supervise the backstage technicians. He accepted on one condition—that Danny (who couldn't sing or keep very good time) agree to be his first assistant. Wise Mr. Barth! He knew that Danny frequently felt left out of class music programs and that the boy needed desperately to "belong." Danny flushed with pleasure and agreed.

5—Still to be worked out: How could these programs be arranged so that children in such a variety of grades would be able to appreciate them? (One idea—mimeograph notes for broadcast, giving each teacher a copy at least one day in advance. In this way teachers of younger children could explain to the class what they might expect to hear. Another idea—have one broadcast just for lower grades.)

6—A *very* important point for the planners to remember: This is like radio, for your audience can only *hear* and not see. Each class listens from the room and will not *see* the performers.

Too much for eleven-year-olds? At times they thought so but were deeply involved and there was no retreat. New problems were met squarely, discussed, pondered—and solved. As Danny said several times with much head-shaking, "I never knew music was fun, but you know what, Mr. Barth? I like music!"

More ideas you can try in your creative music

There are a number of creative music activities that can be used in any grade. A teacher makes the necessary adjustment to suit the age and experience of the children with whom he is working.

1. Compose your own ostinato—vocal or instrumental—to a familiar song. (See Chapter 5.)

2. Compose a descant—or a simple harmony—for a song that is sung frequently. (Chapter 5—vocal; Chapter 6—instrumental)

3. Improvise a three or four measure introduction for an assembly song.

4. Arrange a vocal *and* instrumental coda for a favorite song. (Chapter 5)

5. Write new words or an additional stanza to a classroom song.

6. Write a melody for a favorite poem. (Chapter 7)

7. Make up a story about a recording you enjoyed, for example, Moussorgsky's "Night on Bald Mountain."

8. Paint a picture of a flower as you listen to MacDowell's "To a Water Lily."

9. Use the scale to build a song. (Chapter 7)

10. Use the pentatonic scale to compose an Indian melody or chant or dance. (Chapter 6)

11. Write words and music for a song, basing the melody on varieties of "do-mi-sol-do." (Chapter 5)

12. Make up a pantomime play to accompany Dukas' "The Sorcerer's Apprentice."

13. Act out the story of Grieg's "In the Hall of the Mountain King" from the Peer Gynt Suite #1.

14. Arrange a series of water glasses, partially filled to various depths, in any order. Try composing a tune by striking them gently with a fork or spoon.

THE QUESTION OF MUSICAL CREATIVITY

1—There is much more to musical creativity than the composing of a song. True musical creativity is a broad field that includes the need for some knowledge of simple instruments, arranging orchestrations of these simple instruments, composing descants and ostinatos, planning an assembly program *and* composing a song, too.

2—Every individual is in some way creative but needs to get rid of whatever is stifling his initiative.

3—Creativity cannot flourish in an unfriendly atmosphere, but unless there is some discipline it is apt to go to pieces.

4—An alert teacher can take advantage of any unexpected opportunity to encourage creativity in children.

5—An original idea grows from some interest and flourishes if encouraged.

6—Children need a sympathetic adult to guide their creativity so it is not wasted.

7—There is a happy medium teachers and parents often find which is free of domination and yet realistic. This is the best atmosphere in which to foster creativity.

8—An enjoyment of choral speaking gives children necessary confidence and the desire to create melodies for favorite poems.

9—Planning a good assembly program has many advantages for the individuals in a class and for the group as a whole. It develops the good "belonging to a group" feeling and creative ideas and plans flow more readily.

chapter 8

The Kinship of Music
with Other Areas

We have spoken often of the role music plays in the elementary classroom—how it lends color and relaxation to the school day. Now let's consider how it furthers "Understanding"—the understanding of *people, places, things*.

Children tire of words, whether spoken or written. They hear Teacher talking (often too much, often too loudly). Mother talks—and sometimes nags unthinkingly. The written word? It surrounds the school child's life. Words, words, words! Spoken and written—*ad infinitum*.

Along comes *music* with a different appeal and a smile appears as children sing of a bunny, a truck, a gliding canoe, cowboys, a child their own age in Japan or South Africa—as they dance a Virginia Reel or Hora, sing a swinging chantey or a lively patriotic song, or pound a drum. Children enjoy music—and along with this enjoyment comes the beginning of *understanding*.

Music has been known to unravel a knotty math problem or open the door to a child's interest in science. It can make poetry more appealing or spur the budding artists to greater creativity. It gives children something in common with other people who might have seemed different from themselves. Music is not a panacea for all that may be wrong with us, but it's the nearest thing to it that we know.

Today's great challenge—understanding others

The child today lives in a noisy world of turmoil. Parents can no longer protect their children from its impact. The media bring the best and the worst right past the doorstep and into the living-room. Mother and Dad and Teacher may insist on certain standards of behavior, but the youngster sees and hears these values challenged daily. He wants to know some answers, but how can we provide them when often we don't know either? And if we could furnish the answers to his questions of what's going on, and why, the child lacks the maturity and the background to assimilate such knowledge.

Children from comfortable suburban homes can't possibly understand life in a ghetto. Children living on a ranch can't be expected to feel for the migrant worker. Children watching a TV report from a far-off land are distressed when they see a frightened boy or girl searching the ruins of his bombed-out home, but they can never feel the terror and despair written on the face of the little victim. "Our children shouldn't!" you say. Of course not, but in a world like this they had better *begin to understand*.

We do have something in common with the rest of the world and, great as this "something" is, it can't accomplish the impossible, but it's the best bet we have. Our common language is music—not hate; not guns. Every people on earth, every stratum of our own society, has its music, its own story of everyday living.

Oscar Hammerstein ("the second," as he called himself) with his great insight and his unusual ability to write meaningful lyrics, showed us the way when he wrote "Getting To Know You" into the score of "The King and I." Anna with her middle-class English background grew to love the people in the royal family of Siam and they returned her feeling. Could any two backgrounds be more dissimilar?

George Gershwin, with a background of Brooklyn and Manhattan, was able, through a real interest and understanding, to bring us a picture of Catfish Row with its problems of life and death, its gentle lullaby, "Summertime," and its violence—and make us care. You would not expect Gershwin to choose Porgy and Bess for his hero and heroine, but he did—and he made them real and warm and human.

Music and the social studies

Our biggest concern as teachers must be to prepare the children in our care to live in a small world that is unlike anything we knew at their age. As children, we heard about the need for "understanding" but felt secure in our own communities and, although we sympathized to some extent with less fortunate youngsters, we found it easy to sweep such problems away in a corner.

To say that times have changed would be one of the great understatements of the age. No longer can we afford to let "understanding" and "cooperation" be merely words in a dictionary; they are the stuff of survival.

The social studies program is supposed to concern itself with social relationships—not only the history and geography of a country but the personal relationships of the members of a society.

This is a pretty big order for our children—and for their teachers. We've come a long way from the days when "History" and "Geography" might be taught as unrelated subjects—so unrelated that a class could be studying the history of the United States and the geography of Europe at one and the same time without the curriculum turning a hair. That day is long gone but there's still room for improvement.

We can't expect the elementary school child to assimilate the whole idea of the interrelationships of the peoples of the world, but we can *guide* him in understanding the samenesses and differences in peoples. Here's where our common bond, our common language of music, is invaluable.

The music of any land is a story of contrasts. There is the plaint of the shepherd—and the bold hunting song of his lord. There is the lullaby of the fisherman's wife—and the keening song for a father who will never return. There is the song of the black slave—and the gay dance music to entertain handsomely dressed guests of the plantation master.

In our own land we have the unbelievably wealthy—and disgracefully neglected ghettoes. We have overprivileged, frequently spoiled youngsters—and others who never get enough to eat. We have a "majority," proud of its heritage—and minorities, rapidly becoming the "majority," who are equally proud of a great diversity of heritages. American music has been enriched by each segment of our society bringing its wealth of folk music—and we never seem to tire of listening to this endless variety. What a mistake it would be if we narrowed our listening to that type of music in which we were reared—music that makes us feel at home.

Teachers owe it to themselves, and certainly to their classes, to investigate all kinds of music. TV programs are coming on constantly —programs that bring such entertainment as a festival of mountain music, a combination of gospel and soul music or a jazz quartet that makes a specialty of surprising its listeners with beautiful renditions of old classics.

There is no better time to start a music program designed to improve the understanding of our children than right now. In any large city there are representatives of all the races and countries of the world. Let's see what these people have brought us as their musical contribution to the everyday life of America. We will have to go back a long time in our history to get even a partially complete picture of this musical heritage, but it's an enjoyable journey.

America's earliest music

Our country was never without music. The first explorers and the early settlers found music an important part of Indian life. The less warlike tribes are said to have enjoyed a melodic type of music, singing of crops, moon and sun, and courtship, mostly in what we recognize as the five-tone scale and usually in a descending pattern. The songs were short and to the point.

Indian music was not written down but taught to succeeding generations. The white settler, trying to imitate or notate (write down) the music, was unable to reproduce some of the effects of the quavering notes of a melody. Consequently, it was not until the turn of the century that the phonograph, taken to Indian reservations, captured a few of these songs so posterity might know the true sound.

The late Geoffrey O'Hara, well-beloved composer of some of our favorite songs, was on the Navajo reservation about 1913 trying to record typical Indian music for the Department of the Interior. He told of how difficult it was to determine the rhythm of the songs for it seemed to vary from measure to measure. Thanks to one Indian youth with "infinite patience" (as Mr. O'Hara described him) who sang and played these melodies over and over, the riddle was solved—the music was found to follow a true pattern.

Your class will enjoy Indian music

Small children like to imitate the beat of the tom-tom which was the principal accompanying instrument.

    1—If they thump one of the several homemade drums described in Chapter 6 they'll be able to carry the rhythm needed for a war dance, complete with head-dress.

    2—An original song (written by the class) based on the five-toned scale can tell a child's version of an event in Indian life. Accompany with a regular, soft beat on the tom-tom with the palm of the hand.

Drum beat 1-2-3-4

Corn is grow-ing near the wig-wam; Lit-tle Ea-gle, chase the crows.

    3—Let your older children experiment with original pentatonic (five-toned) melodies using a recorder for the descant. The recorder is not unlike the flageolet type of flute used in Indian music.

    4—Make a "squaw" drum, a "brave" drum and a "medicine man" drum—which they say can forecast the weather. (Refer to Chapter 6 for hints on making drums.)

    5—Send "coded" messages on your drums. Take them outdoors to find out how far the message can be heard.

    6—Try out your drums with the fingers, fist (gently at first), palm of the hand. Experiment with several types of homemade drumsticks.

    7—Combine singing with flute, drums, rattles.

    8—Paint your instruments with Indian designs.

    9—Read stories of Indians in Colonial days and Indians on today's reservations.

    10—Write your own stories about Indians. A poem. A short play.

    11—Is our government doing anything to improve the lot of today's Indians? Why have they been so neglected?

    12—Have the children heard of "Vista"? Could the Peace Corps help?

We see how music can lead the way to all kinds of subjects and discussions. A teacher begins with Indian melodies—which lead to poetry. Poetry and melodies lead us to art, to science, to social problems, to discussions which an alert teacher can guide in almost any grade. Our children are ready to listen, to think, to *understand*. It is up to us to waken their interest.

Music in Colonial America

> I have found from experience that children are deeply interested in the way music developed in our country. They enjoy looking into songs people enjoyed singing, their instruments, their dances. It makes the great variety of national backgrounds come alive as children examine the contributions made by Americans of all colors and nationalities.
>
> For this reason our discussion goes into some detail in describing the music of America from psalms to jazz. I hope your children, too, will enjoy their journey.

Our earliest colonists led a dangerous, strenuous life in which there was little time left for music. Some of them, very religious, felt that instruments were too frivolous for use in the church service.

Psalms were sung at church but, since psalm-books were scarce (and many would not have known how to use them anyway), the good old "lining-out" method was practiced. This is much the way you teach a new song to your class—one line at a time (group repeats it), then a second line (group repeats two lines) and so on until the song is learned. This method worked if the one in charge had a fair voice—and good pitch. You can imagine how *un*musical it *could* become. Gradually the better singers gathered near the front and became the "choir" as we know it today.

As more and more settlers came to the new land they brought their music with them. The songs of the native land were never forgotten and were taught to succeeding generations who carried them lovingly across mountains and deserts and up and down rivers as they moved farther west.

People brought instruments from the old country—of necessity those that were more easily carried, such as the violin, flute and hautboy (from the French "hautbois" which became the oboe). Books of instructions came too, tucked safely away in pockets.

Neighbors formed musical groups for their own pleasure. Some were tiny orchestras—others, singing societies. We find the "singing school" popular in communities and a growing interest in music as people joined such groups for sociability and entertainment.

Organs and harpsichords appeared here and there when the master of a crowded ship could be persuaded to bring them across the ocean. The Germans and Swedes in Pennsylvania used the organ in church, claiming that it improved the singing. In fact, these music-loving people felt that an attractive church service might aid in spreading the gospel to neighboring Indian tribes who, according to organ enthusiasts, would come running from far and near at the sound of such unusual music.

As early as the 1740's the Moravians at Bethlehem, Pennsylvania, presented Bach chorales and by the end of the century, Haydn's oratorios. It wasn't easy to find qualified organists, for the organ is more complicated than one might expect. When an organist could be persuaded to come to America, the congregation often found it difficult to pay the poor man a decent salary and it became necessary for him to eke out a living by teaching music—singing groups and students of instruments being the richer for it.

The gentleman and the lady who had servants (or slaves) and more leisure than their neighbors, were expected to play some instrument well. Trios and quartets met at various homes and passed the long evenings pleasantly together. It was not unusual for these amateurs to perform the works of such great musicians as Handel and Bach. This is surprising for we don't think of music written by contemporaries (1750's) being played then in the far-off colonies.

In the years before the American Revolution music, in one form or another, had found a firm foothold in the new land. There was a sense of belonging when one was a member in good standing of a singing school or a church choir or a little orchestra. Belonging to a group was very much needed by people who worked hard, lonely hours on farms or plied their trade by themselves. Meeting at the church or school for a session of singing with one's friends was a red-letter occasion for folks in small, isolated communities.

Music was hard at work doing its share to create "E Pluribus Unum."

Class activities in Colonial music

1. A volunteer chooses a song to teach class using "lining-out" method. (He will need your guidance.)
2. Listen to a selection from Haydn's "The Creation."[1]
3. Listen to Wanda Landowska play J. S. Bach's "Well-Tempered Clavier" on a harpsichord. The first selection was used by Charles

---

[1] Vienna Philharmonic—London 1271.

Gounod for his famous "Ave Maria." (Victor LM 6801)

4. Can several members of the class form their own instrumental trio? Quartet?

5. Can your class plan a miniature concert of instruments and voices?

6. Ask for volunteer reports on Handel, Bach, Haydn. Use recordings to illustrate reports as suggested in Chapter 3.

7. Find out more about the Moravians—their background in Europe, settlements in Pennsylvania and North Carolina, their musical contributions to America.

8. Are there any Moravians in these sections today? Have they made any later contributions to our music?

The bountiful contribution of Negroes to American music

It's difficult to realize that black slaves were brought to Virginia plantations before the Pilgrim fathers landed at Plymouth. The slaves had little to sing about, but we know from the countless stories brought back from the plantations by visitors and by travelers of earlier days that they very definitely had a music of their own. Some of it surely came from Africa with these people; much of it, no doubt was a blending of the native rhythm with new music heard in new surroundings.

We know the drum formed the background for rhythm. This instrument was often forbidden because the drum could send a message a long distance and this message might bode no good for the white master. But drums there were, made secretly out of whatever material was available. The banjo ("banjer") was a favorite too—often a homemade contraption that served the purpose.

Visiting preachers, stopping at a plantation, held religious services which the slaves were permitted to attend. Here they heard Bible stories that appealed to them of other slaves in bondage, golden chariots, rivers to cross. Visiting missionaries, such as John and Charles Wesley, brought more of these wonderful stories and songs—the "gospel" song with a rhythm begging to be syncopated by people to whom syncopation was as natural as breathing.

Here again we have no actual notation of the songs of the slaves— some of the "spiritual" type; some work songs. There were many notations made by white travelers but they are not accurate because the African Negro slave had a way of slurring some of his notes and flatting others that the white man did not understand. If only someone could have had the yet uninvented talking machine there to record an authentic, truly improvised, unrehearsed, naturally syncopated work song or true, uncontaminated spiritual or a "shout" song[2] or a session of "Pattin' Juba."[3]

The contribution of the Negro to American music has affected all our so-called native music and has spread to the entire civilized world —thanks to modern media. When we discuss the subject of ragtime, blues and jazz a bit further on, we'll begin to realize the greatness of the contribution.

Work songs

In the earlier chapters on "Rhythm" and on "Singing in the Class-room" we spoke of the importance of the work song in building the United States. The rhythm of a song not only makes a job go more quickly but keeps the laborer at a task long after tired muscles beg to quit.

If we look into the music of other lands we'll find the same story whether it's the "Volga Boatmen" or "March from the River Kwai." The rhythm of a song, gay or despairing, has made possible the im-possible. In our own history the types of work songs are largely those of (1) the sea (called chanties or shanties) for the sea was the only life-line between the colonies and the mother countries; (2) of the rail-road and the canal for these were the life-lines between cities; (3) of the cowboy who appealed to the romantic side of the population and, hard as his life was, became a sort of symbol of the world of the great West; and, of course, (4) the work song of the plantation slave for its solace and sheer beauty.

What a wealth of music the work songs and spirituals offer our chil-dren. And what a wealth of "understanding" these folk songs offer if we take advantage of the possibilities they hold for a teacher and class. You have not only songs of valor, romance, sorrow, pride (in a job well done); you have history opened up for the children as these work-ers made the land grow and the seaways shrink. And geography goes along as an inseparable companion to history.

The folk song—and this includes the work song—tells a simple story of ordinary people, and children find these people are interested

---

[2] A spiritual sung with great excitement accompanied by hand-clapping, shuffling feet and swaying bodies.
[3] Not religious in nature. A dance where part of the group danced and the rest stamped and clapped in 2/4 time—usually a fiddler or "banjer" player present.

in and are afraid of the very same things that they are. It's a great step toward understanding when a child realizes that people everywhere feel much the same about life as he does.

In addition to learning and singing many kinds of folk songs, there's a great deal to be gained by probing into the background of the melodies. Older children enjoy the fact that (1) most of the tunes were brought from the mother country and, while (2) the tune was kept pretty much intact, (3) the words were often changed to fit the new surroundings and circumstances.

Another fact, equally interesting, is that deep in our Appalachians, even in this day, there are people whose ancestors settled there more than two hundred years ago who sing and play tunes whose words have not changed. As nearly as researchers can establish, the songs have stayed in their "pure" state in spite of being handed down from generation to generation.

Songs and games for the young ones

Small children enjoy the song-games that youngsters play all over the world. It's a fine time to begin to teach "understanding" by talking with first and second graders about other boys and girls who play these games—some in other schools, other cities, other lands and in other languages.

1—Is there a story about "London Bridge"?

2—Isn't it interesting to know that children in other lands wash clothes, bake, go to church just as the "Mulberry Bush" tells us?

3—How can we find out more about other children?

4—Are their houses like ours?

5—Do they go to school?

6—Are their clothes like ours?

7—Would you like to learn a French song? (Or German? Japanese?)

Let's not neglect songs of our own land that our children enjoy: "She'll Be Comin' Round the Mountain," "Go Tell Aunt Rhodie," "Ding, Dong, Bell."

1—Do you know someone who lives in the mountains?

2—Or someone who owns a pet goose, duck or chicken?

3—How many of you own a pet pussy cat?

4—Did you ever see a well?

There is so much to learn from little song-games.

Patriotic songs

Much as we may not like the fact, most of our patriotic music is a product of wartime. Some of the songs written in past years during periods of national stress are still popular—and one of them became our national anthem. During the Civil War and World Wars One and Two song writers really outdid themselves. Feeling ran high; the people fighting or working for victory were united. One commentary on the unpopularity of the Korean and Vietnamese wars is the scarcity of songs connected with either.

In the days preceding the American Revolution there were few composers in our colonies, although people loved to sing and a number of them could play an instrument. When some new indignity was imposed on the colonists by the mother country, a rash of poems appeared in what passed for newspapers in that time. Occasionally, such a poem was set to the music of a tune already popular and sung on street corners or in taverns. Most of these songs had their moment of popularity and died a natural death.

"Yankee Doodle" was the great favorite of the Revolutionary period and we still enjoy it. "Chester," a song that minced no words in describing the "infernal league of British tyrants" and the "galling chains of their slaves" (the colonists), was very popular and has been called the "Over There" of the Revolution. How many of us have even heard of it? But "Yankee Doodle" is familiar to everyone.

One favorite composer of the time was Francis Hopkinson who had a finger in every pie from writing popular songs ("My Days Have Been So Wondrous Free") to signing the Declaration of Independence. His son, Joseph, is noted for writing the words of "Hail Columbia," to the tune of the "President's March."

William Billings, the fiery patriot who wrote both words and music of "Chester," has been called the first American composer. Most of his music was written for the church and this church music aroused a good deal of controversy. He was dissatisfied with the usual "psalm-singing" in the service and introduced his own style of "fuguing"—not in the style of the great Bach but in the style of William Billings. At least he was original in his ideas for church music. Too bad it could not stand the test of time. Billings' "Fuguing Tunes" are not in use today.

By the 1860's America had become a singing nation and during the Civil War, songs, both patriotic and sentimental, appeared in great numbers to inspire North and South to continue the sad, dreary conflict. The South adopted "Dixie," a popular minstrel show number, for its own. The North took "The Battle Hymn of the Republic" to its bosom. The music of "John Brown's Body," strangely enough, seemed perfectly suited to the magnificent poem by Julia Ward Howe.

"Tenting on the Old Camp-Ground" was written by Walter Kittredge who published a whole book of songs for the Union. George Root composed words and music to "The Battle Cry of Freedom," "Just Before the Battle, Mother," and "Tramp, Tramp, Tramp." "Maryland, My Maryland," "When Johnny Comes Marching Home," "Marching Through Georgia," "The Girl I Left Behind Me," "The Yellow Rose of Texas"—a seemingly endless list of songs was written during this period and many of them are popular today.

Your fourth to sixth graders will enjoy some of these ideas

Youngsters from ten to twelve love to put on plays. Here is your golden opportunity to let them revel in play-writing and planning programs for themselves or a neighboring class or even for an assembly.

The girls can write a scene of Civil War ladies, North or South, knitting, sewing, talking about events in the war and about food shortages. Perhaps they can weave into the story something about the "other" side. One of them may have a brother or son who has joined the enemy's cause, for this happened frequently. Perhaps a tired, wounded soldier appears, begging to be hidden from his pursuers. Perhaps the girls can sing "When Johnny Comes Marching Home."

Your boys may show an evening campfire with tired, home-sick soldiers around it. They talk about the battle just fought or one that may have to be fought tomorrow. Some wear bandages. The guard on duty calls out "Halt!" He drags in a wounded fugitive from the "other" side. Which side? Does it matter? The feelings are the same and so are the hopes and fears. Make this point clear to your young scene-writers and actors.

There is a wealth of songs that can be incorporated into your play. Is there a child in the group who can accompany the singers on some small instrument that could be carried in a soldier's knapsack? It would add greatly to the effect.

And all this time, while children are trying their skill with the written and spoken language, while they are enthused with "putting on a play," *understanding* is working its way into their consciousness with the help of the old songs of the period.

Songs of the two World Wars

The rash of songs of the Civil War period was small compared to the lyrics and melodies that poured out during the period from 1914 to 1918 on both sides of the Atlantic. Many were definitely martial— still more told of the partings and separations of wartime. It's hard to say which were the most popular for we have such contenders as Geoffrey O'Hara's "K-K-K-Katy," George M. Cohan's "Over There" and England's fine contribution, "Keep the Home Fires Burning."

Singers and entertainers visited training camps. Irving Berlin, in camp himself, wrote a musical, "Yip, Yip, Yaphank," for the "boys" to put on for their fellow draftees; a show that helped them forget, for the time, the discomforts of an army camp. "Oh! How I Hate to Get Up in the Morning" brought down the house and let a private get in his licks in an acceptable way.

One of the truly memorable songs that came out of World War One was written in 1919. Gordon Johnstone met a friend of his who had been a sergeant in the Canadian Army and had seen his men wiped out in an attack. "I feel these men are still alive," he told Mr. Johnstone. "They seem to be near me. I can feel their presence."

Mr. Johnstone wrote a poem which he called "There Is No Death" and showed it to his friend, Geoffrey O'Hara, who was greatly impressed by it. For some time Mr. O'Hara tried to find the right music, but nothing seemed to fit these words. Then, one night it came to him. He went to his piano and wrote a song that has become part of our heritage. "There Is No Death" is often played or sung at the Tomb of the Unknown Soldier as part of Veterans' Day ceremonies.

Songs of World War Two

If people thought they had seen a wealth of songs appear between 1914 and 1918 they were in for a new surprise. During World War Two our neighbors across the ocean sang songs to hide their despair of the insurmountable odds they faced. The Aussies brought an old favorite to Europe from "down under" and "Waltzing Matilda," while it was not a war song, nor a marching song, nor a sentimental song, became well liked with the Allies and found its way across the Atlantic.

The British troops in the Libyan campaign adopted "Lili Marlene" for their own. "Captured it from the Germans" was the way they told it.

Oscar Hammerstein (the second) wrote a touching lyric about Paris, then in enemy hands, and Jerome Kern, with his gift for the perfect melody, wrote the music and "The Last Time I Saw Paris" was heard over the radio every day.

Irving Berlin did it again in World War Two. He had written a song a generation earlier for "Yip, Yip, Yaphank" but did not use it. Kate Smith appealed to him for a song she could sing at a patriotic rally. Mr. Berlin remembered "God Bless America," dusted it off, revised it —and we all know the rest.

When asked if he could prepare a new show for this new generation of draftees, his answer was to go to the same camp on Long Island and live there to "get the feel of it again" while he wrote the show "This Is the Army." "This is the Army, Mr. Jones," and "Stage Door Canteen" are two popular numbers from the show.

Burton and Kent wrote a sad little song (sad because it was about a boy living in an England under siege) and "The White Cliffs of Dover" was taken to the hearts of people nearly everywhere. "Comin' In on a Wing and a Prayer" honored the valor of bomber crews with a mean job to be done. The song, "Rodger Young," told of a young soldier fighting in the Solomons who gave his life for his buddies.

New songs appeared almost daily and, as usual, some were short-lived and some may become immortal. Do war songs help us to *understand?* Probably not. War is a dirty business but people, caught up in a war, try to live through it by any means available and the songs they sing unite them—give them strength and the courage they cannot live without. Songs help them to forget, temporarily, a present that is too awful to bear.

How can your youngsters use war songs?

War, unfortunately, plays a large part in the background of people and we can't ignore it when we study the relationships between nations. Rather than extol the glories of conflict, let's try to show our children what their parents and grandparents experienced during such times and how they managed to come through as well as they did.

Some of the children in your classes may have a parent who lived in terror when a youngster; experienced at firsthand what most of us read about. Without dwelling unduly on such subjects, let your children understand that these things happened and let them talk about it if they wish—with you in control of the situation. To pretend that war is anything but evil is stupidity.

Now: time to enjoy the songs that came out of the abyss.

1—Listen to recordings of these songs. Here's another time your Schwann catalog and your music store proprietor will come in handy.

2—Ask your Public Library what albums they have for you. There is an increasing supply of albums for lending.

3—When the children have heard and sung a number of Civil War songs or World War songs, help them plan a "Cavalcade" of a segment of American history, write a simple script and weave favorite songs into it. The show needn't be elaborate but it should carry a message. Let the children decide what this message is to be—with your help, if needed. The high point of the Cavalcade will be the songs.

Costumes aren't hard to obtain. A little research into the dress of previous generations will be fascinating to little girls who become fashion-conscious at an early age. Then too, Mother and Grandmother remember some of those World War One and Two days quite clearly and would no doubt be delighted to assist as fashion coordinators.

Country music

Country music actually did have its beginning in the country and the name tells us something. People in the "country," whether it was mountain, valley, woodlands or desert, had their own music and played and sang it as part of their lives.

Most of the songs are utterly simple. The songs are about work and play, love and hate, life and death. The lyrics are most unpretentious —just tell a story of what happened and when and where. Take "On Top of Old Smokey" or "Folsom Prison Blues"; "Streets of Laredo" or "By the Time I Get to Phoenix"—there is a similarity in the simplicity of each story.

Years ago people in small, isolated communities had to depend on themselves for entertainment. Sometimes they gathered at the schoolhouse or in someone's barn for a hoedown. Here the fiddler was in his glory and there was more than a little competition to determine who could play for the dancing, fast and furious, for the longest time.

Families on lonely farms had their own music. Daddy or Grandpa could make his fiddle if need be and play it very competently. A simple homemade type of guitar, banjo, flute and dulcimer vied with the fiddle for popularity. Some of the songs were from the old country; many were composed here by the musician to fit an occasion.

Country music has always been well-liked, but first radio and then TV have increased its audience a hundredfold. How many years has the "Grand Old Op'ry" flourished? And what of the multitude of country singers presented constantly on TV? (And some of them are *very* good.) There is something about the music that has an appeal for most of us. One of the interesting facts is the speed and agility of these country singers who accompany themselves on the guitar—for this seems to be the favorite instrument. Their fingers fly and the chords present a beautiful harmony for the simplest song.

It has become the custom of TV channels to offer a variety of festivals and we may see and hear this folk music in its native surroundings—albeit a fine arena set in a background of mountains and pastures. There is the unusual opportunity of seeing an instrument such as the dulcimer, or its cousin, the zither at close range so those interested in an ancient instrument can see how it is played. And here again, the playing is perfection.

For your class to try

1—Give the children a store of country music to enjoy. Take old favorites such as "Pop! Goes the Weasel!" Create original square dances—but in order to get the effect you want it's better to use a lively record than to depend on enough agility from a struggling ten-year-old violin student.

2—Select some of the better country stars of TV, such as Johnny Cash or Glen Campbell—and some of their records suitable for children. Teach the song from the recording, as suggested in Chapter 2.

3—Plan a combination hoedown and "sing" using, for example, "Arkansas Traveler."

Our Fiftieth State

For many years we have enjoyed the gentle music of Hawaii as sung by leading crooners on radio and TV. In any song-fest someone is sure to ask for "Aloha Oe" or one of the Hawaiian-type melodies from the movies, such as "Sweet Leilani." There is something restful and satisfying in the rhythm for the singers and for the casual guitarist or uke player.

We are fortunate to have a singer who calls Hawaii his home—lives there and is happy to raise his children in that land. He extols the beauties of the country, yet is very much aware of the changes taking place. Don Ho is an artist who understands Hawaii's history, lives actively in Hawaii's present and looks forward to a great future as a citizen of the fiftieth state.

Don Ho makes many recordings but there is one I would like, especially, to recommend for your class—Reprise–RS–6303, named, appropriately, "Hawaii—Ho!" Here he talks to his listeners, quietly, about the music that came with the New England missionaries— hymns, of course. You hear one sung in the formal New England manner and then you hear how the natives took the song and made it their own by changing its rhythm to that of the Islands. It gives insight into the gentle nature of the Islanders who didn't fight the influence of the missionaries but simply fit it to their own needs.

Another interesting part of "Hawaii—Ho!" is Don Ho's invitation to youngsters to pick up spoons, cereal boxes—whatever is at hand— and create their own rhythm band to accompany a song. Your children will enjoy listening first to the effect produced in the recording and then trying their own rhythm instruments while *they* accompany Don Ho's music.

Latin-American music

The music of our neighbors to the south and in the islands of the Caribbean has delightful rhythms to offer us. There is something about this music that one cannot resist for it sets hands and feet in motion almost before we realize it. The instruments used in Latin-American melodies are perfect for the job they do—indeed, everything about this music is perfect.

Take the Tango—probably the earliest of the Latin-American rhythms to attain great popularity with us up north. Although it was first a Negro drum dance, it became a ballroom favorite usually considered Argentinian in origin. The Tango is spirited and graceful, beautiful to watch and fun to try. The rhythm with its marked

$$\text{♪. ♪♪ ♪ | ♪. ♪♪ ♪ |}$$

is pleasant and uncomplicated for children to understand. They love to beat it out on drum or desk or make up a simple song to the satisfying rhythm.

Brazil has given us the Samba which is also African in origin. Its 4/4 time is beaten 1-2, 1-2 (duple time) and is now mostly a ballroom type of dance.

From Cuba and neighboring Caribbean islands we have the delightful Rumba (Negro in origin) with its strong rhythmic syncopation and duple meter. Who can turn a deaf ear to a melody with the beat of

There is no catchier rhythm than that of Calypso music which is also in African style and is usually a ballad type of song of the West-Indian Negro. In Chapter 3 we spoke of Harry Belafonte who has made Calypso music quite different from that which the tourist hears on a Caribbean cruise. His ballads vary from a love song such as "I Do Adore Her" to the wistful "Day-o" of the tired banana-boat loader— one that your boys would certainly enjoy singing. Give the girls the opportunity of accompanying with the rather unusual drum effects. (Victor LSP—1248-e.) When you preview the album—always a must—you may find a ballad not suited for young ears. It's an easy matter to skip over that band of the record.

Here is a tiny sample of "Pack She Back to She Ma,"[4] an amusing little ballad about a sweet little girl who couldn't— or wouldn't— bother to cook. Both girls and boys will enjoy the banter—the exchange of good-natured raillery—as the girls sing their own version with, "Pack he back to he pa . . ."

Oh, pack she back__ to she ma,   Oh, pack she back__to she ma

It should make us stop and think of the tremendous debt American music owes the Negro when we realize that these Latin-American rhythms we enjoy are directly connected with the African beat and syncopation that came with people forced to labor in lands not of their choosing. Whether the slave was taken to the islands of the Caribbean or the mainlands of North or South America, his music went with him and became part of the heritage of those lands.

---

[4] Words and music from: H. Wilson, W. Ehret, A. Snyder, E. Hermann, and A. Renna, *Growing With Music—Book V* (Englewood Cliffs, N.J.: Prentice-Hall, Inc., 1966).

The beginnings of jazz

Some insist it began in New Orleans—others, St. Louis. But this we know: the cities along the Mississippi provided work for the freed Negro and wherever he went he took his gift of song and his love of the syncopated phrase. To any adopted music, to any music he sang, he gave a "hot" quality, ragged it, strongly syncopated it, embellished it with improvisations and was thoroughly successful in creating an exciting new form of music.

At the close of the Civil War, used army instruments flooded the market and could be picked up cheaply. The music-loving black worker who had made do with shoddy or homemade instruments now had an opportunity to get a decent one for himself. What better time to use this cornet or drum than at a funeral? The body was respectfully escorted to the burial ground with appropriately solemn music but on the return trip the mourners felt free to let go. The crowd that joined the parade filled the street, cheering on the band, dancing, singing. Players and followers worked up an awful thirst, so they frequently spent the next few hours in local taverns where the music and gaiety continued.

New Orleans is the city usually connected with all this, but there is no reason why other cities cannot lay claim to like situations. The "ragged" time, or "Ragtime," flourished wherever the black man settled and interest in it became a craze and spread like wildfire. Then the piano joined the brass (indoors, naturally, and usually in a sort of honkey-tonk setting). Ragtime pianists became as adept with the instrument as the cornetist, trombonist, banjo-player or drummer with his. Piano ragtime was a syncopated melody played over a regularly accented 2/4 time in the bass. It is commonly believed that Irving Berlin's "Alexander's Ragtime Band" started the craze, but actually the song came in at the end of ragtime's reign which lasted from the 1880's to 1914.

Birth of the Blues

The spiritual may be the Afro-American *choral* singing, but the blues is the Negro singing *solo*. It is a simple story, just as the white man's folk song is simple but follows a definite form, although the singer may improvise as much as he feels the need of it. Line one is the statement, repeated once and then again for emphasis. Line four is the introduction of a new thought, then repeated. Line six is the response to lines four and five. Let's take an example:

> Wish I was a little child again,
> Wish I was a little child again,
> Wish I was a little child again,
>   An' my mama take me by the han',
>   An' my mama take me by the han',
> "Don' cry, my lil chile!"

Any blues was not sung "straight" for it was full of improvisations, slurred notes, flatted notes, frequent exclamations such as "Oh Lord!" or "I say!" It started as a lament for the lot of the black man or woman and worked its way to music halls and supper clubs where the melody was enhanced by the addition of musical instruments. The piano filled in any empty spot in the blues song with flourishes of notes, chords, scales. The trombone seemed to echo the singer with a wailing voice.

William C. Handy is often called "Father of the Blues," although he did not originate it, for the blues probably started in the cotton fields or along the wharves. He was born in Florence, Alabama, in 1873 to the family of a Methodist preacher. In spite of a disapproving father, the boy composed his own songs and often made his own simple instruments. This gifted musician and composer seemed to have the ability to take the music so familiar to him and to his people and produce a "Blues" that their white neighbors could understand—and imitate. His "St. Louis Blues" and "Memphis Blues" are known world-wide. A statue of William C. Handy stands in the park named for him in Memphis, Tennessee.

Ragtime, blues and jazz are closely interrelated and it's hard to say where one stops and the other begins. Jazz is definitely for musical instruments and seems to be the attempt of the instrument to imitate the blues singer—a difficult feat with the necessary slurs and flatted notes so important for the true effect of the voice.

The jazz musician takes a melody and weaves his own improvisations into and around it, changing the feeling of the musical phrase. The blues singer does the same thing as though both he and the instrumentalist had some great need to express.

Neither jazz buffs nor blues buffs can agree on the relative merits of the black and the white performer. Did the white musician get his inspiration from listening to the improvisations of such greats as Gertrude (Ma) Rainey? Bertha (Chippie) Hill? Louis Armstrong? Blind Willie Johnson? Could any white singer possibly have equaled the feeling and beauty of "O Lord, Take My Hand" as Mahalia Jackson sang it at the burial of Martin Luther King, Jr.?

The real question is, "Does it matter?" If a gifted singer has "soul," whether he is black or white, whether he sings blues, gospel or opera, he is able to carry away his listeners on wings of song. A true musician, no matter what instrument he plays or what type of music, whether he is a black trumpet-player or a white trombonist, if he puts his own soul into his playing, the listener responds.

Jazz is America's musical gift to the world and has been accepted in foreign lands more readily than in the land of its birth. Our modern composers recognize the appeal of jazz and no longer hesitate to incorporate its very attractive features in their classical compositions.

Should your class hear jazz?

It would be a mistake to play only classics for your children's appreciation just as it would be wrong to play only ragtime and the blues for them. Folk songs and patriotic songs are their rightful heritage— and so is jazz. You want them to hear and understand the works of the Masters just as you present a background in any subject. Would you hesitate to bring history up to date in the classroom? Then why the hesitation to let a group of young Americans hear Louis Armstrong and his trumpet? Or Mahalia Jackson and her golden voice? Or King Oliver and his Creole Jazz Band?

There are record albums to help you here. Other teachers have felt the need of guidance in teaching something "different" and recording companies are responding. You will find a wealth of material listed in Folkways/Scholastic Records free catalog. Why not order one for yourself from—

> Folkways/Scholastic Records
> 906 Sylvan Avenue
> Englewood Cliffs, N.J. 07632

There are three albums of jazz to get you started—(1) *The South,* which traces the origins of jazz in Negro folk music from "field hollers" to rag and blues; (2) *The Blues,* featuring Blind Willie Johnson, Ma Rainey and Bessie Smith; (3) *New Orleans,* in which you will hear street band music, a spiritual in New Orleans style and Louis Armstrong and "Jelly-roll" Morton. There are several other albums in this collection of jazz treasures which are listed in the free catalog above.

Small children might not be ready to enjoy these records—nor would your ten- to twelve-year-olds without some background preparation. Begin with stories of the old South—the black slave, the plantation, the sorrows and the occasional festivities. Help the children see a picture of the black man and his life in this period of slavery. Help the children understand how, slowly and painfully, a new form of music was taking root. Teach them some of the songs, give them the opportunity to hear many others. I know of one group of ten-year-olds who wrote some blues about a rainy day and about a coming test they didn't want. Don't put a jazz recording on the turntable and sit back and expect results. Teach this as you would any other subject—from the beginning.

How fast you go and how far is something only you can judge. It is important that the children understand *one* feature at a time and have the chance to explore it and enjoy it. Be wary of playing wild sounding rock records. Not only do today's children hear this and see rock groups much of the time, *but* they may get out of hand and then you'll have yourself some trouble. *If you know your class* and are acquainted with their background in popular music and if the perfect opportunity presents itself—then, good luck.

Music is everywhere

Music and the social studies fit like hand and glove. They are made for each other. But let's look, even briefly, at some of the ways music can help us teach other areas of the curriculum.

If one tries to list the ways in which music helps in the understanding of another area of study, the biggest problem is, "Where do we begin?" Is it possible to separate music from—*anything?* All through our previous chapters we have discovered how closely music is integrated with living—how perfectly it weaves itself in to produce a perfect unit of study. We have seen its correlation with other areas—its mutual relationship to literature, painting, the physical well-being of relaxation, how it stimulates creativity. Music seems to be the magic catalyst that unites not only areas of study but people too.

Perhaps the best way to discuss the close relationship of music with other studies is to look into a few concrete examples of how it has worked in actual classroom situations. Teachers have to be practical people and the pragmatic John Dewey tells us that an ounce of experience is worth a ton of theory.

Peggy's fractions

Peggy is an average ten-year-old girl. She can be very wise at the most unexpected times—and completely silly at others. She loves to read, plays the piano quite well, despises math.

Peggy's classroom teacher says the math trouble stems from a complete lack of interest. Peggy's music teacher finds his pupil is able to sight-read well but never bothers to consult the time signature before plunging into a new "piece."

It is the custom in this school to have festivals and to invite a talented outsider to perform at them. Sometimes a parent sings a song of her native land or a father brings his accordion to accompany a dance. In this case the festival was to be presented by the fifth and sixth grades. There would be Latin-American dances and songs by the sixth grade and Colonial music and square dances by the fifth grade.

And it was at this festival that Peggy's school teacher and Peggy's music teacher met for the first time, for the latter had been invited to play some Mexican numbers as a special treat for the audience. Peggy was thrilled by this because she is very fond of both these teachers.

At the end of a delightful show, Peggy managed to bring her two teachers together. After the usual pleasantries the topic of their mutual interest was mentioned. They agreed about the little girl—capable, careless, affectionate. So she doesn't like math? Hm-m. Then maybe that's why her only difficulty with music is the time. But when she gets into the spirit of a new selection she has no trouble—seems to fall into the specified rhythm almost automatically. Could be that her good sense of rhythm carries her along.

It was agreed that the music teacher would crack down on time signatures and insist that Peggy study each time signature before starting any piano selection. She must learn that 4/4 time means the *equivalent* of four quarter notes in a measure and that there could be two half notes or a half note and two quarter notes—and so on. (A most practical way to study fractions.)

The class teacher plans to team Peggy, the music lover, with Frank, the class math whiz kid, whose attitude towards music is "Who needs it?" They are to prepare a chart for the bulletin board that will list the class favorites in songs. The chart is to show (1) a tiny staff with time signature for each song, (2) conductor's beat for song, (3) composer and (4) book in which each song may be found. To decorate this chart the two young specialists will feature the several time signatures their classmates should recognize, such as 6/8 which might have *six eighth notes in a measure* or *three quarter notes* or *two dotted half notes,* and so forth. They will consult at regular intervals with their class teacher *and* Peggy's music teacher.

Frank is amused by Peggy's difficulty with such simple details as fractional equivalents and Peggy is appalled by Frank's lack of interest in music. They should be good for each other.

It challenged even Ben Franklin

Everyone likes to tap a water glass. Fill it halfway—then tap it. Drink some of the water—tap it again, and listen to the different tone. All ages get pleasure from the simple experiment.

Billy and Dennis, our experimenters from Chapter 6, are no exception. They love to tinker in their fathers' garages or their mothers' kitchens. Billy is the idea man and Dennis the bookkeeper—and this is a fortunate combination. Billy gets the inspiration, he and Dennis experiment and the careful Dennis keeps a running account of successes and failures in his school notebook.

Their fifth-grade class read a story of Benjamin Franklin— —not the usual story of his arrival in Philadelphia nor even an account of his famous kite and key. This story told of Mr. Franklin's interest in music and his invention of something he called a "harmonica" or an "armonica"—not the kind we know today but something that Dennis and Billy just had to try. The whole idea is based on water glasses, so that's where they started.

Here's Dennis' account of a succession of experiments which the boys helped their teacher decipher so the class might benefit from the boys' trial and error method of approach:

"Billy and I read that Benjamin Franklin invented this 'harmonica' thing and liked it so much he wanted to have some way of carrying it around so he could play it anywhere. Glasses with water are pretty hard to carry around, I guess. Anyway we had to start the experiment with just the glasses and the water before we tried anything fancier.

"We didn't want anyone else fussing around, but Ralph (he's on the science committee) said we'd better let him in on the experiment or it wouldn't be legitimate—or something like that and I guess he knows because his father's a lawyer. Then Katie said there should be a girl working on it and she'd be a good one because her father runs one of these variety stores and she could get us lots of glassware. It's a good thing we let her stay.

"Here's what we found out:

　　1—Glasses are all different sizes and make different sounds.
　　2—More water makes a glass lower in sound.
　　3—Less water makes the sound higher.
　　4—If you want to play a scale you have to keep changing the

amount of water in each glass until you have all the tones from low Do to high Do.

5—If you need sharps or flats in your song other glasses must be tuned and added.

6—We used my little sister's xylophone to get the right pitch.

7—Ralph said the water would evaporate overnight so we marked the level of each glass with my mother's lip-stick.

8—Katie tried tapping the glasses with a knife blade (no good), with a fork (much better), with a spoon handle (the best).

9—We had to let my little sister play a tune and she broke one glass and tipped over another. That's where our bad luck began."

There's a pause of several days in Dennis' story. He told his teacher there was so much going on he couldn't bother to write it down. Briefly, this is the story:

When the young scientists had repaired little sister's damage they decided it would be wiser to keep the experiment in the classroom. What better time to take Ben Franklin's idea of a carrying case and put it to practical use? Ralph contributed a small, battered suitcase and Katie a roll of heavy plastic tape and "six more glasses—just in case."

There was the tricky problem of fastening each glass securely so it would rest on the bottom of the suitcase. Since this was impossible without emptying the water, they did so, reluctantly. When the feat seemed to have been accomplished and the tape and glasses fairly secure, it was unanimously decided to take the experiment to school the next morning.

Dennis carried the suitcase with all the respect of a demolition expert defusing a bomb. Billy, Katie and Ralph surrounded him to run interference if necessary. There was one hair-raising moment when Dennis' aching arms relaxed their grip but the tape and battered suitcase lock held and the day was saved.

Dennis wrote in his notebook: "It turned out all right because our teacher said we could work in the classroom and then all the others could see what was going on and maybe come up with a good idea for keeping the water from spilling out or evaporating. The kids are interested in what our committee did and, anyway, we plan to use this 'harmonica' thing to make up tunes or maybe play a descant."

An Indian drum that forecasts the weather

This experiment was tried in a third grade—and in a sixth grade with a few more elaborations. (See *Make Your Own Musical Instru-*

ments by Mandell and Wood.[5] In this book you will find many more experiments in music-science with flutes and pipes and stringed instruments.)

The medicine man would have used a hollow log covered with untanned deer skin. The pitch of the drum varied by wetting the skin or scraping it dry. Medicine men are said to have awed the tribe by forecasting the weather. If the sound from the drum was dull it meant rain. If the beat sounded clear the weather would be fair. It's fun to experiment just to see what happens.

In lieu of hollow logs and untanned deer skin, your children can try a galvanized pail ¼ full of water. Cover the pail with a piece of chamois or canvas or heavy linen and bind securely with a wooden hoop or a wire. Give the surface a *thin* coat of shellac. Get the drumhead good and wet by swishing the water inside the pail. Play it while wet. Let it dry and try it again. Keep a record of your successes in forecasting weather.

Your good readers can help by doing extra research for the class

1. Using a committee of four good readers and two artistically inclined class members, plan a mural of (*a*) ancient instruments such as the harp, psaltery, timbrel, cymbals, lyre, dulcimer; (*b*) history of the piano; (*c*) people and instruments in history and in fable who are associated with music—Orpheus, Pan, Hermes, Jubal and David from the Bible.
2. Have two of your good readers (or high IQ children) help class librarians make a list of books in which there is material available to assist in preparing reports on composers, instruments, the fugue, the blues, and a host of other music subjects.
3. Ask for volunteers to keep a scrap-book of clippings brought in by class members on any interesting musical happening. A looseleaf book will be more practical since similar topics can be kept together. See that the book is indexed as much as possible.
4. Make a small group of good readers responsible for checking music sections of newspapers and magazines for articles on current happenings.
5. One child should be responsible for checking TV magazines to keep teacher and class informed of coming programs of interest *and* the date and time.

---

[5] Published by Sterling Publishing Co., Inc., 419 Park Ave. South, New York, N.Y. 10016, 1968.

MUSIC COMES TO LIFE IN THE CLASSROOM

1—In a world with a superfluity of words—spoken and written—the appeal of music is universal.

2—Music helps bring an understanding of people, places and things. It is the nearest we know to a panacea for all our ills.

3—Music is the world's common language. It enables children and adults to understand the samenesses and differences of people in our own land and in other lands.

4—American music has been enriched by the folk music of each segment of our society, past and present. Singing and playing this great variety of music helps children to understand others—and today, more than ever, *understanding* is necessary to survival.

5—The study of American Indian music brings up the question of the Indian of today—and our neglect of his problems.

6—The study of the music of our earlier colonists shows the need these people had of being able to sing and play instruments in groups. Through their music they became more united in spirit.

7—The black man's gift to American music is inspiring to black and white alike. From the songs of the slave have come some of our most moving music and syncopated rhythm, blues and jazz.

8—The songs of the working people in America's history help us to understand the feelings and way of life of these laborers who contributed so greatly to the nation's growth.

9—Patriotic songs and songs of the nation's wars show us how Americans have kept up their courage in times of stress by singing together.

10—Each period in American history offers rich opportunities for your children to discover how people managed to exist through hard times and what they enjoyed doing when times were better.

11—We study the music of Hawaii, our fiftieth state, and that of our Latin-American neighbors and come to the realization that their music has become ours also because it has an appeal for everyone.

12—Syncopated rhythms, blues and jazz are contributions of black Americans whose ancestors brought music from Africa and wove it into our "native" music until it has become America's musical gift to the world.

13—Poetry, literature, history and geography, even science and math, are interwoven closely with music. Indeed, your class discovers that music is literally everywhere.

chapter 9

Using Audio-Visual
Aids in Classroom Music

An imaginative teacher always used "aids" of some kind and devised his own when none was available—but that was before modern miracles changed everything. In the Space Age it is shortsighted to deprive teachers and children of the modern media that so greatly enrich the learning process.

A few years ago teachers thought they were doing quite well in audio-visual aids if a school had a few special features like a tape recorder, a TV set and a movie projector. It was frustrating that these treasures had to be shared among so many classes and we dreamed of the day when there might be *two* TV's in the building. A good deal of time was wasted in carting the desired "aid" to one's room or in taking a class to the school's AV center. Classes often "doubled up" but the two-in-a-seat idea left much to be desired.

Teachers and parents are becoming more vocal in their demands and are getting results. What we have now is not enough, but the quantity of teaching aids has increased and the quality and effectiveness have improved greatly.

It's exciting to read the ads in teachers' magazines describing the latest equipment in the AV field. You think, "Now, if I had that snappy new overhead projector (or that new set of transparencies or a cassette tape recorder) my troubles would be over!" And yet you know better. Teaching aids are priceless *if* they (1) *are used and not stored away in a supply closet,* (2) are used *intelligently* by teachers to enrich an area of study, (3) *are kept in repair.*

Since we're discussing music, let's look at some aids in the music field. Let's examine closely some of the old tried and true friendly aids to see if we're using them to full advantage. Let's examine some of the more recent additions to the list also and find out what they're supposed to do for us; if they are what we *really need* to improve our music; if they are *practical, easy to use, reliable.* Remember that a good deal of hard cash will have to be spent for an up-to-date AV aid and it should be what we really need.

How to make full use of the old tried and true AV aids

Radio: It's hard to believe that having a radio in one's classroom was, at one time, quite an innovation.

There are advantages in having a radio available if the teacher consults program guides. A reliable news program when you want it; your local "School of the Air" presentations (if you have FM); some background music (selected thoughtfully)—all these are yours to use.

If your school has a public address system—a mixed blessing— you probably hear some of the "School of the Air" programs broadcast over the PA. But problems often occur: (1) it's out of order, (2) the monitor is absent—or forgets—, (3) it's turned on too late, (4) it's poorly tuned. So if you have your own FM radio you're independent.

Record player: Music educators insist that each classroom should have its own record player and that it remain in that room. If this daydream ever comes true it will prevent your not having the machine when you want it and it should result in fewer repair bills. Carrying equipment around the building doesn't do it any good.

To buy anything but a *good* three-speed record player is a waste of tempers and money. In one school the PTA members of the first and second grades presented the teachers with tiny three-speed players—one for each of these classrooms. The parents meant well but the whole project was a disaster from the start. Someone found "a good bargain" and it was bought and delivered to the first and second year classrooms. The tone was awful; the machines broke down with disheartening regularity; some good records were ruined by faulty needles.

As we have discovered in past chapters, a dependable record player is one of your most valuable aids in teaching music whether you're an accomplished musician or a teacher feeling her way through the music program. We need it for rhythms, for teaching a new song, for background music or for guided listening, for making the acquaintance of the instruments of the orchestra. Ideally it should be at hand when we want it and *must* be dependable.

If your record player is equipped with earphones and jacks it makes a wonderful listening center (in your library corner or music corner) where two to four children may use it without disturbing the rest of the class.

Filmstrips: The faithful little filmstrip projector can help you in any area of teaching. It has certainly proved its dependability through the years and the number and quality of available films is amazing. It's easy to use and rarely requires anything more than a new bulb.

How can it help you in teaching music?

1—Reading music: There are filmstrips that show your class a large, clear staff so everyone can learn its secrets under your guidance. The first film of this set of four discusses the relationship of rhythm to half and quarter notes; the second explains measures and whole and eighth notes; the third, dotted notes and rests; the last of the series explains time signatures.

Preview the film. Depending on the individual class, you may prefer to explain the pictures yourself or choose to employ the help of the accompanying records. One advantage of doing your own explaining is the chance it gives children to ask questions.

There is another filmstrip set that is slightly more advanced. Here we find the study of the staff, major and minor scales and key signatures.

For the fifth and sixth grades there's a set of filmstrips introducing musical instruments and describing how they are made, the history of their development through the years and the use by individual players or as part of a band or orchestra.

All these filmstrips have records that can be bought to be used with them for illustrating the sound of each instrument alone and in combination with other instruments in a quartet, band or orchestra. They do an excellent job.

2—Using the slide attachment: It is likely that your projector has an attachment for showing 2″ by 2″ slides. Although these slides are easily available, you will get a great deal of satisfaction (and save money) if you make your own. It isn't difficult and children like to help—and they learn something at the same time.

Clear or etched glass makes good slides. Have it cut and take the precaution of binding each 2″ by 2″ with narrow tape. Use one of those handy felt pens and there you are! Make your own staffs, G clefs, time and key signatures—or let the children do it. Print your own two line songs. All this can be washed off and the slide used again.

Send for a *free* catalog

If your school does not have a recent catalog of the equipment available from the Society for Visual Education (SVE), why don't you—or your AV coordinator—send for it? In this free catalog you will find hundreds of suggestions for improving the school's AV center. It covers all areas from math, to music, to health. Write to—

> Society for Visual Education
> 1345 Diversey Parkway
> Chicago, Illinois 60614

Some "taken-for-granted" aids to teaching music

The chalkboard: This old faithful doesn't need to boast its modernity. It's old-fashioned but has proved its worth a thousand ways. You'll never find the chalkboard out for repairs. Many times a day this aid is used, erased, used again, washed. Are you planning a new unit of work? Want to list some questions? Solving a math problem?

And what of music? Are you creating a new melody? Jot down the sequence of notes before you and the children lose the inspiration. No time now to get out equipment. The staff-liner (another useful music aid) can come later, but get the quick little notes jotted down now. Words for that new creation? Get them on the ever-patient old chalkboard. It's always *there* when you need it.

The bulletin board: If room permits, keep a separate bulletin board for music. Decorate it with a variety of musical notes, a G clef, some time and key signatures and be sure to change items of passing interest frequently.

What should go on the music bulletin board? Your "Song Bag" (Chapter 2), pictures of famous composers and modern musicians, a child's extra fine report on some matter of musical interest, a clipping from a newspaper telling of a new recording, an account of a musical happening. Where do we find room for all this? Select the best, change it frequently, use a monitor who considers his job of prime importance.

If a separate bulletin board is simply out of the question, use a section of the general bulletin board—but have one. It's worth sacrificing something else.

Music books: In Chapter 4 we discussed the introduction and use of the *music reader* and found that its value in teaching music increased once children had sufficient background to understand staffs, note values, measures and signatures.

It's a good idea to have on your own desk copies of several other music readers—not only from other grades but from a variety of series. The constant use of *one* music reader is boring to children and to their teacher, too.

Perhaps you can remember when music readers were full of insipid little songs about pumpkins and about birdies that went "tweet-tweet." It was unthought-of to include something gay like "A Bicycle Built for Two" or a vivacious Israeli dance tune or a sad, sweet folk song like "Aura Lee." Now something has startled music book publishers into doing more daring things. Could it be the entry of a new breed of publishers into this sacred field? The newer music readers are delightful.

There are biographies of famous composers written specially for the ten- to twelve-year-old reader. They are interesting, sympathetic accounts of the successes—and heart-breaking failures—of people who wrote some of the world's greatest music. Usually the story begins with the composer as a child—which captures the attention of a young reader—and takes the reader on an exciting musical jorney.

Have a talk with your local librarian and find out what she has available for your class. There should be some of this type of biography in your school library and you will find it satisfying to add a few to the library corner in your own classroom. Children love them and the personal interest taken in the musician inspires children to find out more about the man and his music. If reading the story leads to an oral book report, help the reporter along with some recordings to be played for added interest.

The magic puppet: These delightful little creatures enchant all ages for they seem to have the quality of making one believe they are *real*. It doesn't seem to matter whether a puppet is an elaborate work of art, an intricately manipulated marionette, a little doll stuffed with cotton or a tiny finger puppet—they're enchanting.

Want to teach a new song in a different way? Take two hand puppets and, with you, the teacher, supplying both voices, have *them* discuss the possibility of teaching such-and-such a song to the class. (Can you use *two* voices—like Shari Lewis, for example?) Watch the faces of the children. They can't *wait* to hear the new song.

Do you have to be gifted or highly trained to do this? Not at all. Buy (or make) two little creatures (animals, people, like or unlike), plan a simple script, practice at home in front of a mirror. It's not hard to manipulate hand puppets. Perhaps you'll reach a level of accomplishment where your puppet can pick up a pencil and beat time. Before you know it, the children will be begging for a chance to teach a new song this way—or review an old one from the "Song Bag."

Have you a child in your class with a lovely voice who is too shy to sing in front of the room with a small group? Try the effect that a decorated paper bag has on him when he becomes a puppet by the mere placing of the bag over his head—with cutouts for breathing and seeing, of course. The shyness is gone. He may giggle a little but listen to him sing!

Use a puppet to encourage good breathing habits in singing or to practice with off-pitch singers. Plan a little show with two puppets, one teaching the other to sing on pitch.

Joining others in song

We know the joys and satisfactions of classroom singing. There is a feeling of good-fellowship and relaxation when everyone joins in—the good voices, the ordinary run-of-the-mill voices and those that have little to offer but are having a good time.

Singing in the assembly hall can be a boring experience or a delightful event. Lucky are the children who have a lively director and a good pianist. Do you know that some children *never* sing anything interesting or challenging? That they repeat the same old shop-worn stuff week after week in classroom and assembly periods—and are scolded and nagged if they don't respond with some semblance of enthusiasm? Think of all the joyous opportunities lost to them.

Is assembly singing an aid to the teaching of music? It certainly should be—and it can be. But how dependent we are on the people in charge of it.

I have in mind two schools. Shall we call them "A" and "B"? Each found itself with an assembly problem. Let's see how they solved them —it may help you and *your* school if you are in the same boat:

> *School A*—Mr. Lewis is no concert pianist but he can play anything by ear, has a perfect sense of timing, fills in with surprise scales and arpeggios that delight youngsters.
>
> He has been playing in the school assemblies for several years and now he has taken a transfer to a junior high school, leaving a very empty place at the piano.
>
> Miss Delano has been drafted, under protest, to pinch-hit, but she's no good at the piano and knows it. Poor Mrs. Brown, who led the music while Mr. Lewis played, is plain discouraged. There's little response from the children—and no wonder.
>
> How the problem was solved. Mrs. Silvio, newly arrived in the neighborhood, came to register her two boys. In passing the auditorium she heard sounds of music. Being an out-going person she came in and sat down to listen. (A slightly unorthodox approach.) The poor pianist, struggling at the keyboard, was near tears and the director about ready to throw in the towel. Sympathetic Mrs. Silvio with her usual direct approach offered to take over. She played, the children sang like angels and everyone had a fine time.
>
> Is it working? The principal had a few qualms but said, "Give it a try." Mrs. Silvio is delighted with the "assignment"—says she's glad to have something interesting to do, now that her two boys are in school all day. Miss Delano is greatly relieved and Mrs. Brown, who thought she could never work with anyone but Mr. Lewis, has plans for a Sing-o-rama in December and perhaps a music festival in May.

There are talented outsiders in most communities who could contribute a great deal to the music programs in schools. They are not licensed teachers so the school systems don't use their ready help. What are we afraid of? Rather than let a fine, enthusiastic musician touch our pianos we deprive children of the joyous experience of a good sing-a-long. Does one have to produce a license before he can *give* his services to a good cause?

School B—Have you ever been in a school (as student or teacher) where the music was flat and joyless and uninteresting? Where each assembly period was a dud? Where there was never a festival of dancing and singing? Rather dreary, wasn't it?

A new music supervisor came to District 12 and found School B the dreariest of all. She made discreet inquiries and discovered that it had been this way as long as the senior teachers could remember. Dreariness was an accepted way of life.

"Do you like it?" she asked.

They shrugged. "We have no musical talent here. What's the use?"

Miss Gordon, the new music supervisor, asked the principal for permission to call a meeting of the staff. She knew better than to force a program of music, so she presented a well-thought-out plan to the group:

1—A good, new, three-speed record player would be made available from Headquarters.

2—Four fine albums would be given to the school along with the record player—one of chanteys, one of spirituals, one of country music and one of patriotic songs.

3—She, herself, would train a volunteer in the best way to present these songs to the assembled classes. In fact, she would be there to start the program going.

4—Another volunteer would be needed to prepare the words for projection on the screen in the assembly hall, and a third volunteer to supervise the projector.

5—The principal rearranged program schedules to make time for a practice assembly each week. During this practice time the children would learn a new song and review one or two old ones until there was a repertoire built up.

Miss Gordon got her volunteers and the school got its record player and albums. The music-hungry children and their teachers, too, are beginning to have a little fun. The singing isn't all that good but things are on the way up.

Some familiar aids—and improvements being made on them

The Movie Projector: The 16 mm sound projector is difficult to move about the building, so its use is ordinarily restricted to the projection booth. This means that *you* go to *it* for your movies. There's a time loss and the inconvenience of moving a class back and forth. The projector can be wheeled on a stand but this is not ideal, either. It's expensive to buy and repair. If you have tried to load the machine and get the film properly threaded while keeping an eye on a group of restless children, you are acquainted with the problems connected with the use of this teaching aid.

Did we use it? *Do* we use it? Certainly. A movie is just what's needed to lay the groundwork for a new project, to enrich the project or to tie up loose ends when the project is almost completed.

There is available now an 8 mm projector with a cassette loader. No more fumbling or threading or rewinding. The film loop is in the cassette and you—or a child—can slip it into the projector. This machine is compact and completely portable, and a fraction of the price of our old 16 mm.

The Overhead Projector: The old opaque projector has yielded its place to the smaller, more efficient overhead projector. We still have a warm place in our hearts for the old machine but have fewer "bugs" to contend with now. The newer projector is more portable, doesn't require a darkened room. You can sit at your desk and face the class while pointing out whatever you wish to explain by means of a pencil in your hand. This is an improvement over standing with a long pointer in the hand and shuttling back and forth between screen and projector.

There is an increasing number of prepared transparencies available to use with your lessons, but most teachers prefer to prepare their own, whether it's a map, a flower seed or a staff and signatures. The manufacturers suggest using an "angled" screen for best results. This prevents a picture appearing larger on the top than on the bottom.

Tape Recorders: Here we have the same old story of past years when there was *one* huge tape recorder in the building. It was so exciting to use that we lugged it around anyway—which didn't help the machine at all. We were taught how to thread the tape and re-wind it and in the process many a good tape recording was unintentionally erased.

Newer models came along, easier to carry and with a better tone, but we still had the threading and re-winding problems.

Have you seen the new cassette tape recorders? They are *very* portable and easy to use in a music program. The tape recorder has been a boon to teachers in such areas as speech improvement

and choral speaking. When it comes to music we wonder how
we got along without it. Here are a few of the many ways it can
be used to aid and enrich your music:

    1—Record a song as the children sing it. Re-play it. En-
courage critical listening. Sing it again and record it. What's
your opinion? Improved? What part needs more practice?

    2—Teaching a harmony part? See Chapter 5 for ways in
which the tape recorder comes to your assistance.

    3—Record an original song with voices and instruments.
Play it as a treat for parents at the next meeting.

    4—Record a descant so there will be no danger of forget-
ting just how you worked it out.

    5—Record on tape a music broadcast as it comes over the
radio.

Television: The TV set is not new to the school but our biggest
problem with it has always been that there were not enough
of them. If we want to use the wonderful programs that most of
the large cities provide for their schools, it usually means traipsing
around the building with your class. You must leave your room
in plenty of time to be seated in front of the TV set before the
program starts—for it doesn't wait for anyone. Even if there is
more than one TV set in the building the problem is still there.

    It sounds pretty silly to say that children should be encouraged
to watch TV at home. Perhaps we can encourage them to be more
selective—but it won't be easy. There are fine programs youngsters *should* see and sometimes when we question a class next day
we find that only a handful watched some TV gem planned for
children. Too bad.

    Try this:

    1—Use a volunteer committee of three to watch newspapers
and magazines and select (under your guidance) coming
programs interesting to children—a musical fairy tale, a
voyage under the sea, an animal story, a children's concert.

    2—In a prominent place keep a list of what's coming up for
the week. Talk about it with the children; discuss what they
might see and hear; make careful note of channel and time;
see that this is written in notebooks.

    3—If a fine weekend show is coming along, advertise it well.

    4—Follow up with a discussion. Occasionally, ask for a
short paragraph.

    5—Make sure your children watch space shots at home or in
school, depending on the time.

6—A helpful magazine—
Teachers Guides to Television
P.O. Box 564
Lenox Hill Station
New York, N.Y. 10021

Living music

Seeing and hearing an artist on TV can be a rewarding experience. To see him and hear him in *person* means even more. Perhaps there is an aura about a concert hall or theater that we do not find in our own living room. Whatever it is, we know there is an excitement connected with a *live* performance that is missing otherwise.

Have you ever asked your youngsters if they have been, in person, to a concert? Try it some time. Has your school ever had a *live* string or woodwind quartet come to entertain the children—to show and explain each instrument separately and then play a musical selection written just for a quartet? Has a real live violinist ever come to an assembly to talk about his violin—how it's made and how the bow is used? Did some child's mother ever come to show her native costume and sing a folk song of her homeland?

With some thought and planning any number of treats can be provided for the children in your school. Talk with the principal about the possibility of forming a committee to look into this neglected area. Don't be discouraged if the perennial bugaboo about "outsiders" shows its silly head; there's always someone who fears anything new and progressive. And again we ask, "What are they afraid of?"

Your own community has more talent hidden away than you would ever think possible and it doesn't matter what its economic level may be. It's a recognized fact that slum areas have produced many of our ablest entertainers. Is there any reason to think this is no longer so? Have you heard a gospel quartet recently? Do you realize that excellent guitarists are springing up all around us? Let's use some of this available talent to inspire our youngsters with the hope that they, too, can do the same.

Using your school talent

A sixth grader who's studying the violin will enjoy bringing his instrument into your classroom to permit the smaller children to see, at first hand, what a violin really looks like. Perhaps two or three at a time can gently touch the fine polished wood, look closely at the strings and the bow. Then your visitor plays something simple for his audience.

The teacher who plays the piano for assemblies might be persuaded to take a group of children into the auditorium to make the acquaintance of the piano. It too, has strings, but how different! Touch the fine wood *very gently;* press a key. We'll open the top of the piano and you watch the "hammers" while the keys are played. Shall we sing "Oh! Susanna" while you stand there and watch the hammers move?

Jim, in fifth grade, plays a drum in the school band. Invite him to visit your classroom and show the youngsters what a real *band* drum is like. Perhaps he'll let someone try holding the drumsticks—there's a *right* way to do it. Then he may play his drum while the class marches around the room.

All this firsthand information means a great deal to children.

Let's take a trip somewhere

It's a red-letter day when a class goes to visit something interesting. Small children stay pretty close to the school building and they can get quite excited about traveling to the auditorium to hear the Glee Club rehearse for the coming festival. They may have an invitation from Class 2–3 to come and see their exhibit of rhythm instruments and may be allowed to touch or play a drum or a tambourine.

I know of a fourth year class that wangled an invitation to visit a neighboring church building whose organist had agreed to explain the wonderful workings of a pipe organ. One by one the children were permitted to peek *inside* the organ at the amazing conglomeration of pipes and to examine the manuals and foot pedals. Before they left, the organist gave a short concert, explaining in advance of each number what the children would hear.

Fifth and sixth graders can arrange with the museum to see a display of ancient instruments—or perhaps limit it to an examination of the ancestors of the piano.

If you plan an excursion to a museum or to a classroom, make all necessary arrangements well beforehand to make sure you are expected—and welcome. If someone is acting as your guide, try to consult with him before the actual visit. In this way he knows what you want your class to see and will make his plans accordingly. If the children carry pocket-sized notebooks and a short pencil they'll be able to take notes.

Now, go and have a fine time. Perhaps you can plan to attend a concert together sometime in the future.

AUDIO-VISUAL AIDS LIVEN A MUSIC PROGRAM

1—In the Space Age teachers need all the help they can get to widen the horizon of an area of teaching.

2—Audio-visual aids are priceless if they are used intelligently—and kept in good repair.

3—Many of the more familiar aids to teaching music can still be used effectively in today's schools.

4—The record player and filmstrip projector are reliable and useful. Watch for ads in teachers' magazines that explain the newest improvements in these.

5—The overhead projector, used correctly, is a great help in teaching children how to read music.

6—There are many ways in which a tape recorder will improve your classroom singing.

7—Use puppets in your music lessons to create interest. They teach many facts in a delightful way.

8—Assembly singing helps the music program, *but* it can be *a joyous experience* or *a bore.*

9—Consider the many possibilities in your own school and community for making music come alive for children.

10—Plan a class visit to a museum or consider going to a concert.

IN CONCLUSION

Music has more to do with living than any other art but it's treated like a stepchild. It's shunted aside in the elementary program to make room for math or language or science. There's a place allotted to music on the planned program and it's printed in letters just as large but often is taught when convenient and nothing more demanding appears.

And who teaches it? Too often it's the harried class teacher who wants to do nothing more than sit down and be quiet after a rough math lesson. She eases her conscience by having the class run through a worn-out, very small repertoire of familiar songs. This is better than *no* music for it gives the children a little relaxation and a change from the grind of a regular lesson. But is it fair to the children to treat what is probably their most meaningful heritage in this way?

Music and the classroom teacher

There are teachers who have a natural love of music and want to share it with others. These are the people who *should be permitted and encouraged* to instruct their own classes—and other classes on the grade if possible. It is not important that they be highly trained in the intricacies of harmony and counterpoint. It is unimportant that they be good pianists or have outstanding voices.

I remember an elementary school teacher who almost never sang because she felt her voice was poor and she couldn't play more than a few chords on the piano. But she could teach music! One of the best glee clubs in the county was trained by her. This teacher's class presented musical plays. Its understanding and enjoyment of music grew continuously. She directed the assembly music with outstanding success. She attended opera and concerts, took "in-service" courses and evening courses at the university—was "wrapped up" in music. She knew the enjoyment it gave her and wanted the children to enjoy it too.

Then there's Mr. Sheppard. At first he was unwilling to teach his own singing because he had a very deep bass voice. Someone, 'way back, had told him it would be difficult for children to sing with him because of the greatly different range of voices.

One day Mr. Sheppard felt an irresistible urge to sing a favorite passage along with the recording of a swinging chantey. The children listened with delight and honored him with a round of applause. If there's anything a good chantey needs it's a deep, male voice. The ice was broken and he's been singing ever since.

The music supervisor

If you have the kind of arrangement under which a music supervisor comes to your school four times a year, no one has to tell you that it's unsatisfactory. The supervisor does the best he or she can in dealing with thousands of children, but there's time for little more than illustrating some point before a small group of teachers in an assembly hall crowded with classes.

Occasionally the supervisor squeezes a staff conference into the busy schedule, but that means some other school will have just so much less time given to its problems. Material is left in the school for teachers to read (and when do we get around to it?); new books may be left for teachers to try out for selecting a new music reader for their classes; or the supervisor might take pity on a youthful appointee who is scared to death at the prospect of tackling music and give her special help. It's nobody's fault—just seems part of the plot against giving music its rightful place in the curriculum.

What can the principal do?

An elementary school principal doesn't have to be a musicologist to improve the teaching and appreciation of music in his school. He *does* have to be aware of the importance of a good music program—of the lifelong boon it can be to the children under his supervision. He *can* do a great deal but it requires as much thought, planning and dedication as managing any other part of the school program.

If the music program is below average, it shows immediately. What does the principal hear as he walks about the building? Young voices and rhythm instruments and record-playing fill the halls with sound. Which classes seem to be having a good time? Which of the teachers are playing and singing right along with their children? What of the assembly period? A visit or two will tell plenty about director and pianist. He looks, listens, asks a few discreet questions, has some conversations with good musical possibilities on the staff, puts two and two together.

When Miss McClain was assigned as principal to a new school still under construction she asked many a question, had many conversations with teachers interested in moving to the new school. Being a politician by instinct, she knew how to find out just what she wanted to know.

Music was high on her list. She knew its importance to the morale of teachers and children alike. She must have a music teacher but wanted the *right* one. Degrees, color and religion meant little to Miss McClain. All she wanted for her intermediate classes was someone who could teach music well.

From the time the new school opened, Miss McClain gave music first priority—a most unusual arrangement. Was time needed to practice for a festival? Did a record player need repair? Had the pianos been tuned lately? She saw to all this. Music flourished in such an atmosphere. Impressed by the singing and playing in the middle grades, the first and second grade teachers asked that one of their number, the most musical, be put in charge of teaching and leading the singing of the lower grades. Each teacher would handle the rest of the music instruction on her own.

When these small children reached middle grades, they brought with them a fine musical background.

Looking ahead—trends and hopes

The most pressing problem in supplying good musical training to school children is the lack of competent teachers. Old-timers in the system often "get by" with a little knowledge and years of accumulating experience. *This is not enough.* The difference between a person who has a love of music and a "feel" for teaching it and a person who struggles along as best he can is sadly evident in the results achieved.

Some teachers are born with the ability to put music across and make any music lesson an adventure. They are the people who should teach our music, special license or not.

Training teachers

Part of the problem can be solved by giving more attention to the musical training of students in teachers' colleges. They do get some courses in music and observe a class occasionally but, according to these young people, they feel no assurance in their ability to teach music when they graduate.

Some years back, when the public was appalled by our inability to put math and science across to the children, steps were taken—and fast —to improve the situation. What was done to improve the teaching of music? You and I know the sad answer. If anything, music was more neglected than ever for now math and science would save mankind.

Music educators are well organized at present and have more than a fighting chance to bring about some long-needed changes.

"On-the-job" teachers

What of the person who's a good, hard-working, capable teacher and would really like to do a better job with his classroom music? Has he a chance to improve his techniques? When more training was needed to bring himself up to date with newer procedures in math and science, he took courses, in-service and others, until he felt competent.

No teacher can afford to mark time in music and continue to do a good job. There are books to be read, lectures to attend and practical experience to be gained in order for you to do justice to the children. Music is their right but the whole concept of music instruction is changing.

See what your own Board of Education offers in its in-service courses. These are often given by music supervisors and sometimes by an alert, capable, plain, ordinary teacher who knows a great deal about the subject and lives with it every school day.

I recall watching a teacher in an actual teaching situation—actual, except for the fact that it was presented to a large group at an in-service course. The children were learning to read music and made the same mistakes as your class and mine. We learned more in a half hour of watching someone work with a class than we would ever have learned from a lecture on the subject.

There are excellent films of classroom situations. The best of these films are *not* pat, prepared lessons by an expert but show teacher and class making an error and correcting it, trying and failing and trying again—even as you and I.

Ask your supervisor to recommend such a film to be shown at a grade conference. The film can be re-run so the teachers watching it are able to pinpoint some common problem. What did the teacher do when this happened? How did the teacher handle that tricky situation? What would *I* do differently?

Team teaching in music

This seems an ideal arrangement. The person best equipped to teach a subject is the one who does it. Frequently team teaching and non-graded classes go hand in hand. Then we get the benefit of an ex-

perienced teacher working with classes where children have like ability
and interests. Age matters little. The talented third-grader can study
music with others older than he and is able to move along at his own
rate of speed. Quite a change from the run-of-the-mill school where
one teacher handles all subjects and children are herded together—the
slower students too often holding back and discouraging the initiative
of the more gifted.

Talented outsiders

Educators have been a bit stiff-necked about letting anyone but a
licensed teacher come into the schools. All around us, in any type of
community, there are people able and willing to share their knowledge
and gifts with our children—and their teachers, too. Like everything
on earth, this is changing—slowly. There's much reluctance to be
overcome but we're on our way.

Here and there we find a school board employing musicians who
work part time in orchestras or who teach an instrument. These talented
people are pleased to add to their income by coming into the schools at
regular intervals and teaching a group of young hopefuls. Sometimes
it's the guitar or the accordion. Here and there you'll find the owner
of a music store who will instruct interested youngsters in the electric
organ. The school would be unable to provide such equipment and
teaching, but with the community's help it's becoming a reality. If a
child is interested in learning the guitar he doesn't care to be handed a
flute. If the electric organ appeals to him we don't try to satisfy the
urge by suggesting the trumpet.

These "outsiders" (who do much more good "inside") are helping
to make music a living force for the enjoyment of all.

The "Good Gray Poet" knew

Walt Whitman always had his finger on the pulse of America. He
knew what the common man was like—what made him tick—and
knew that music was part of his life. He listened to him, talked and
lived with him. No doubt he sang and played with him too. His beautiful poem, "I Hear America Singing," should be as much a part of our
music program as the patriotic songs of our land.

I HEAR AMERICA SINGING

I hear America singing, the varied carols I hear,

Those of mechanics, each one singing his as it should be blithe and strong,

The carpenter singing his as he measures his plank or beam,

The mason singing his as he makes ready for work, or leaves off work,

The boatman singing what belongs to him in his boat, the deckhand singing on the steamboat deck,

The shoemaker singing as he sits on his bench, the hatter singing as he stands,

The wood-cutter's song, the ploughboy's on his way in the morning, or at noon intermission or at sundown,

The delicious singing of the mother, or of the young wife at work, or of the girl sewing or washing,

Each singing what belongs to him or her and to none else,

The day what belongs to the day—at night the party of young fellows, robust, friendly,

Singing with open mouths their strong melodious songs.

Walt Whitman (1819–1892)

Index